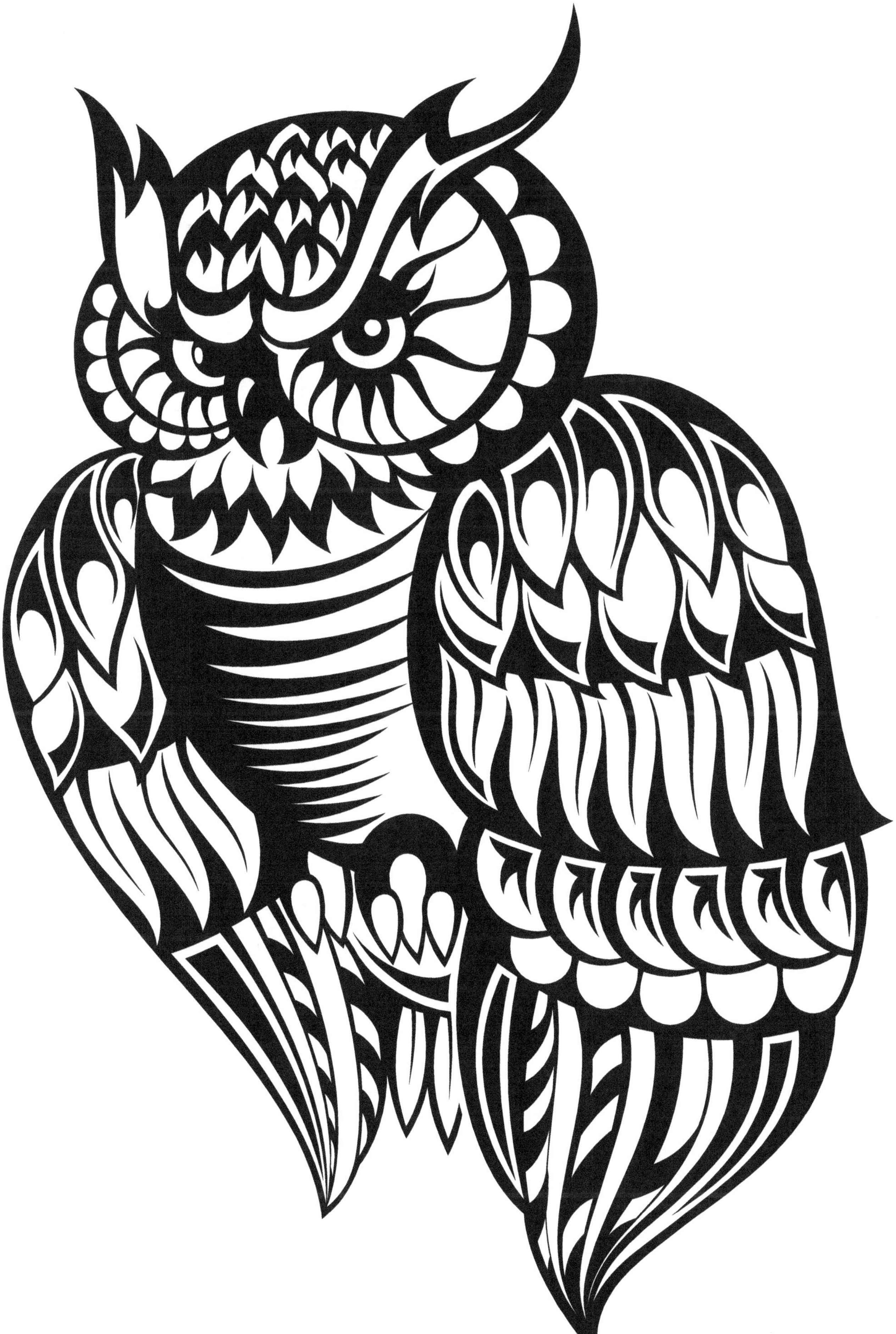

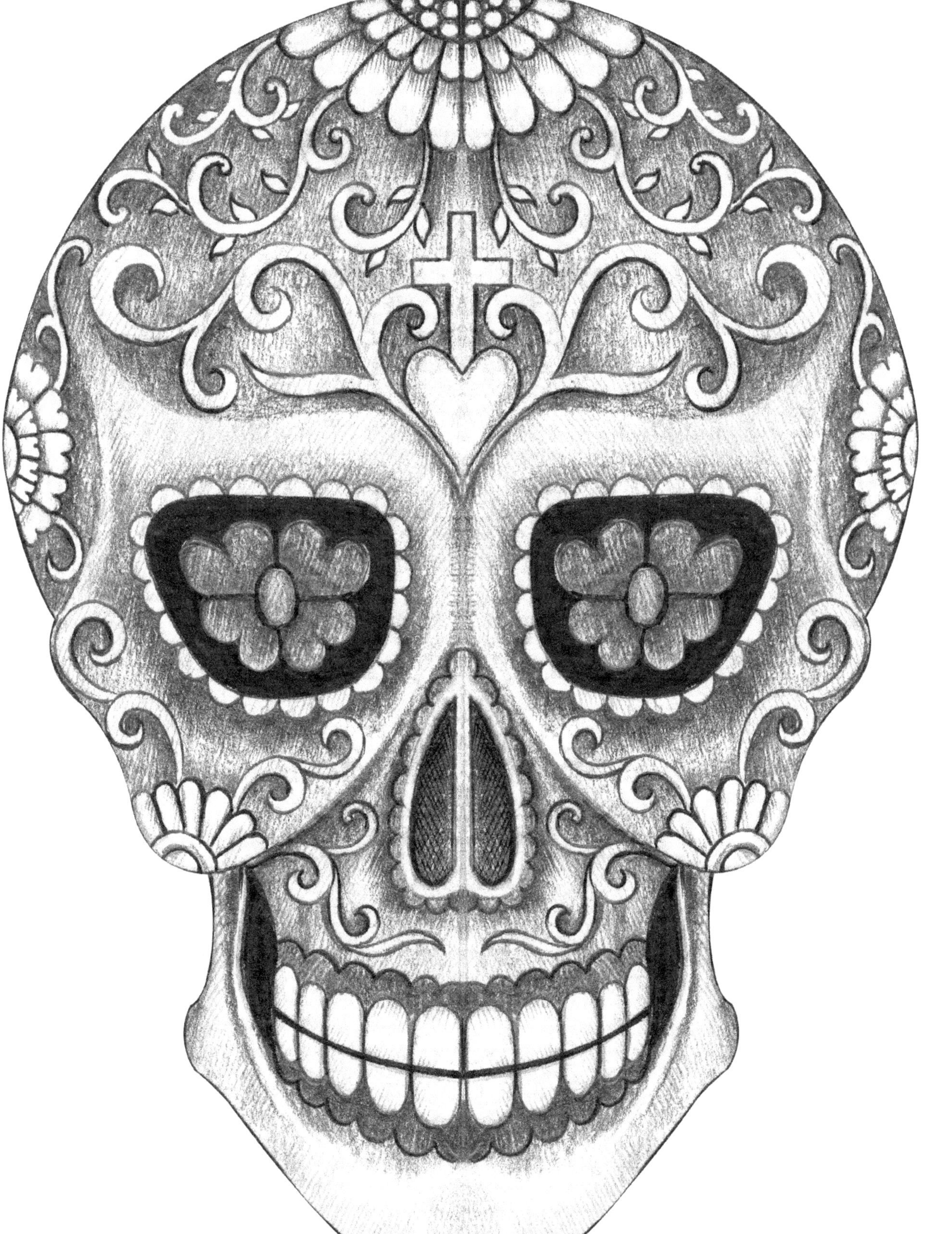

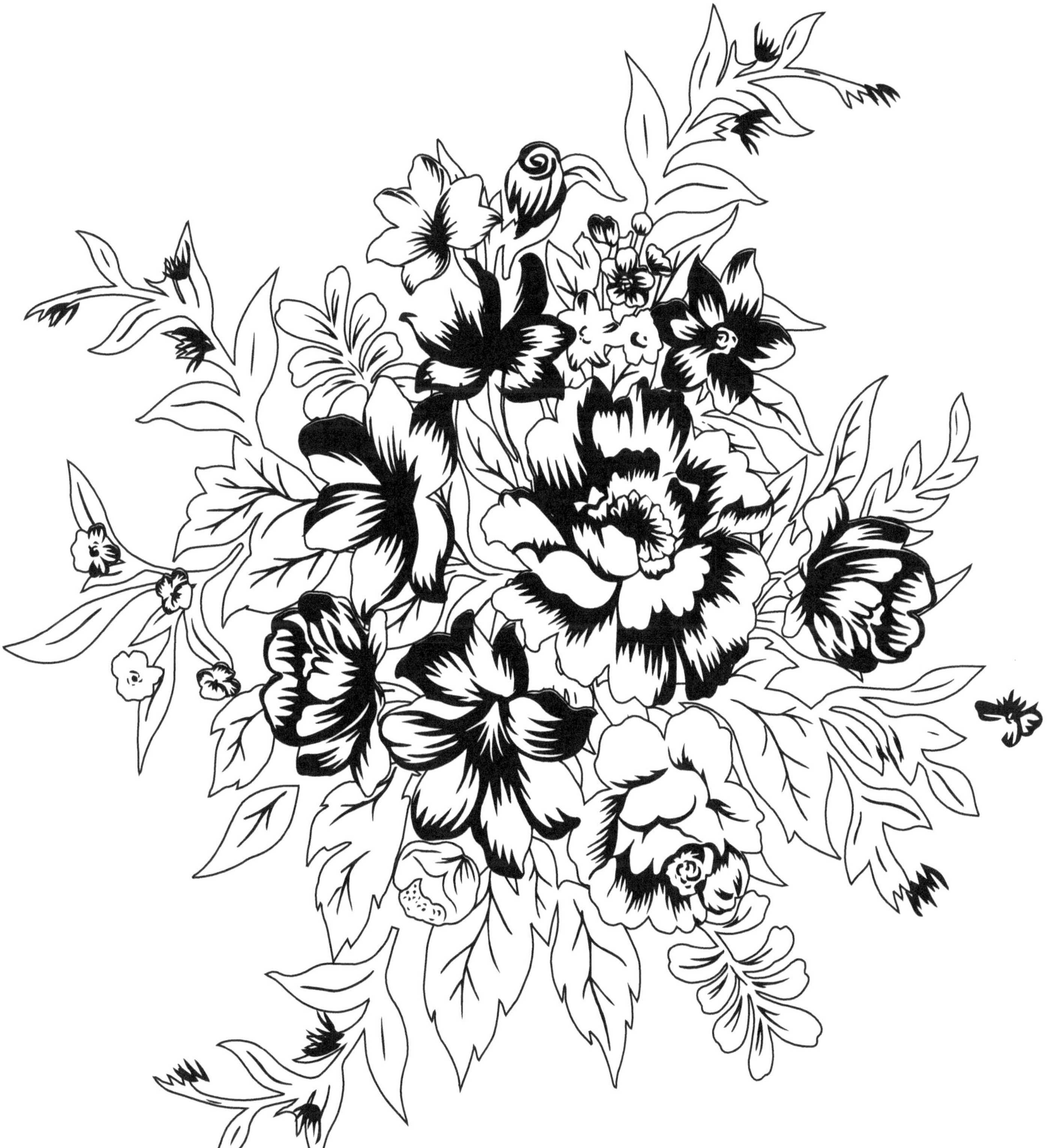

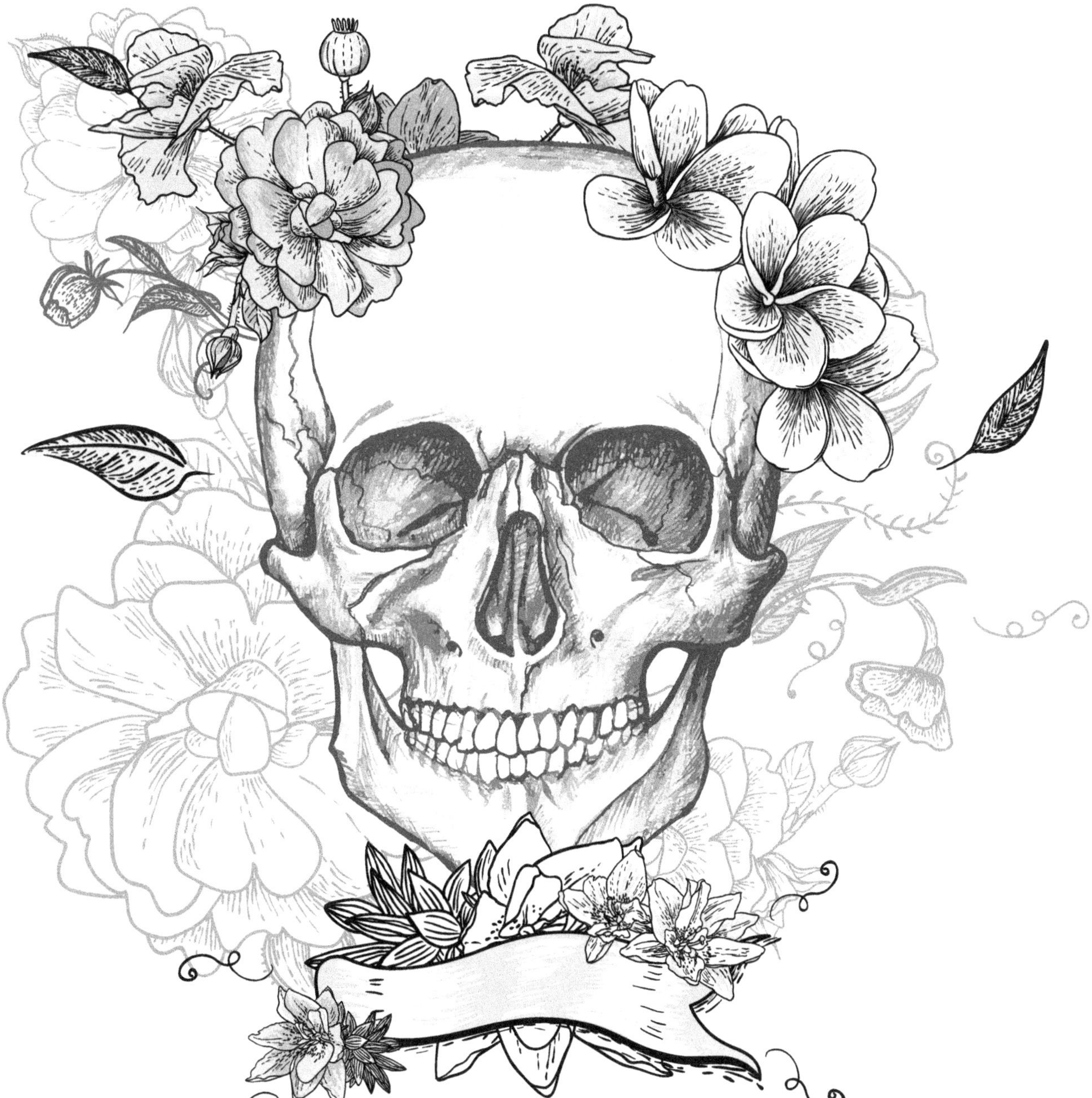

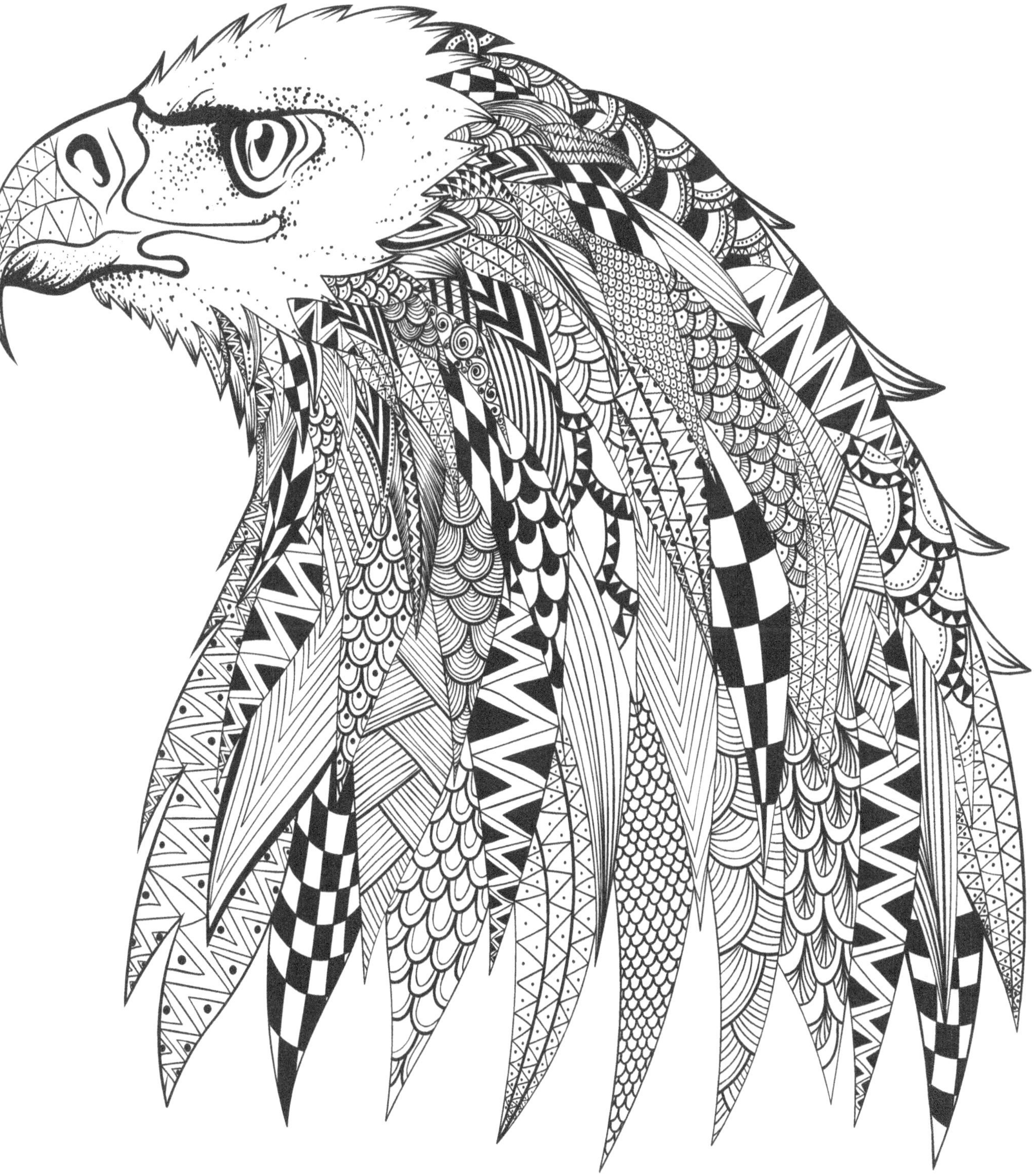

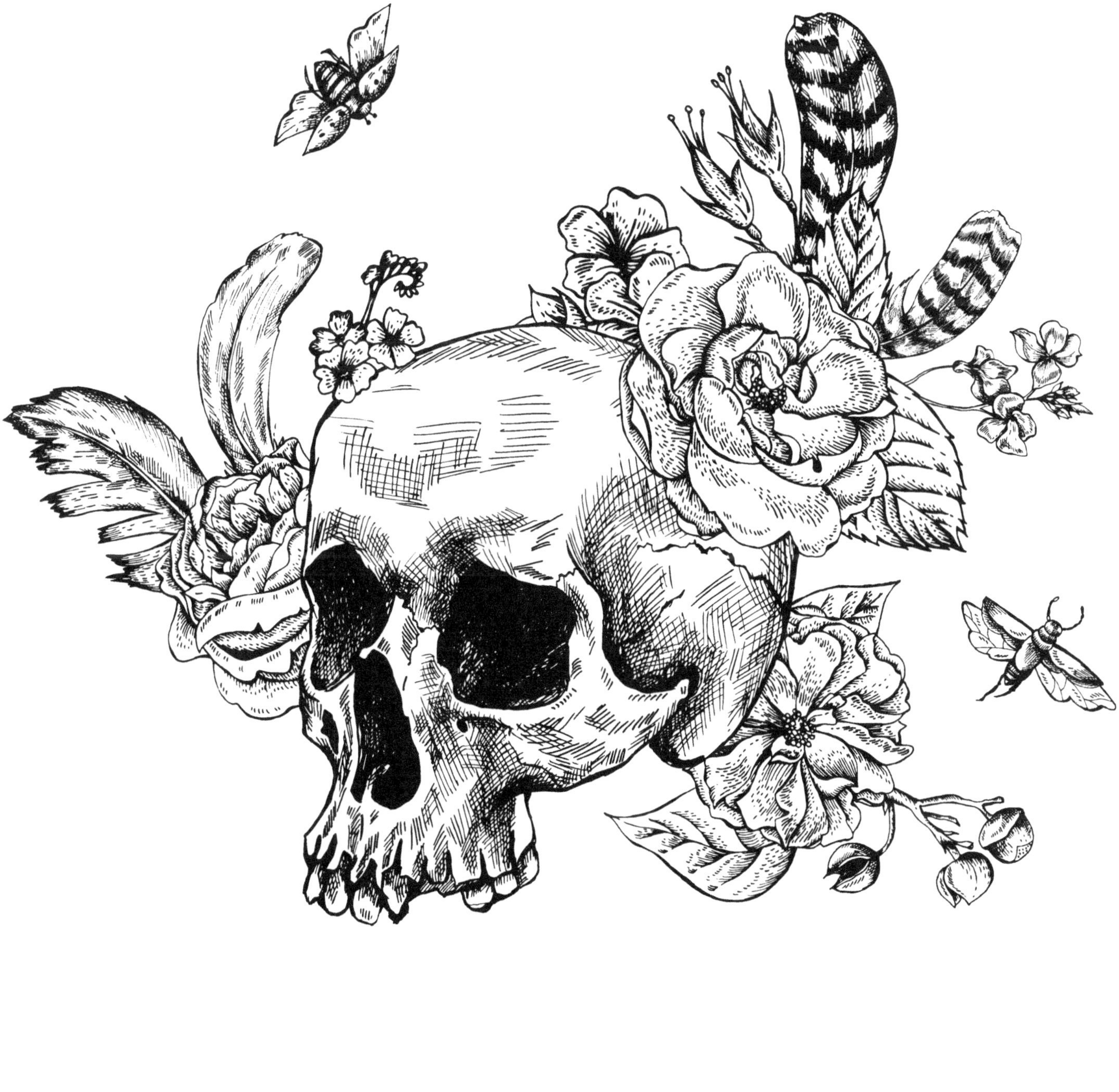

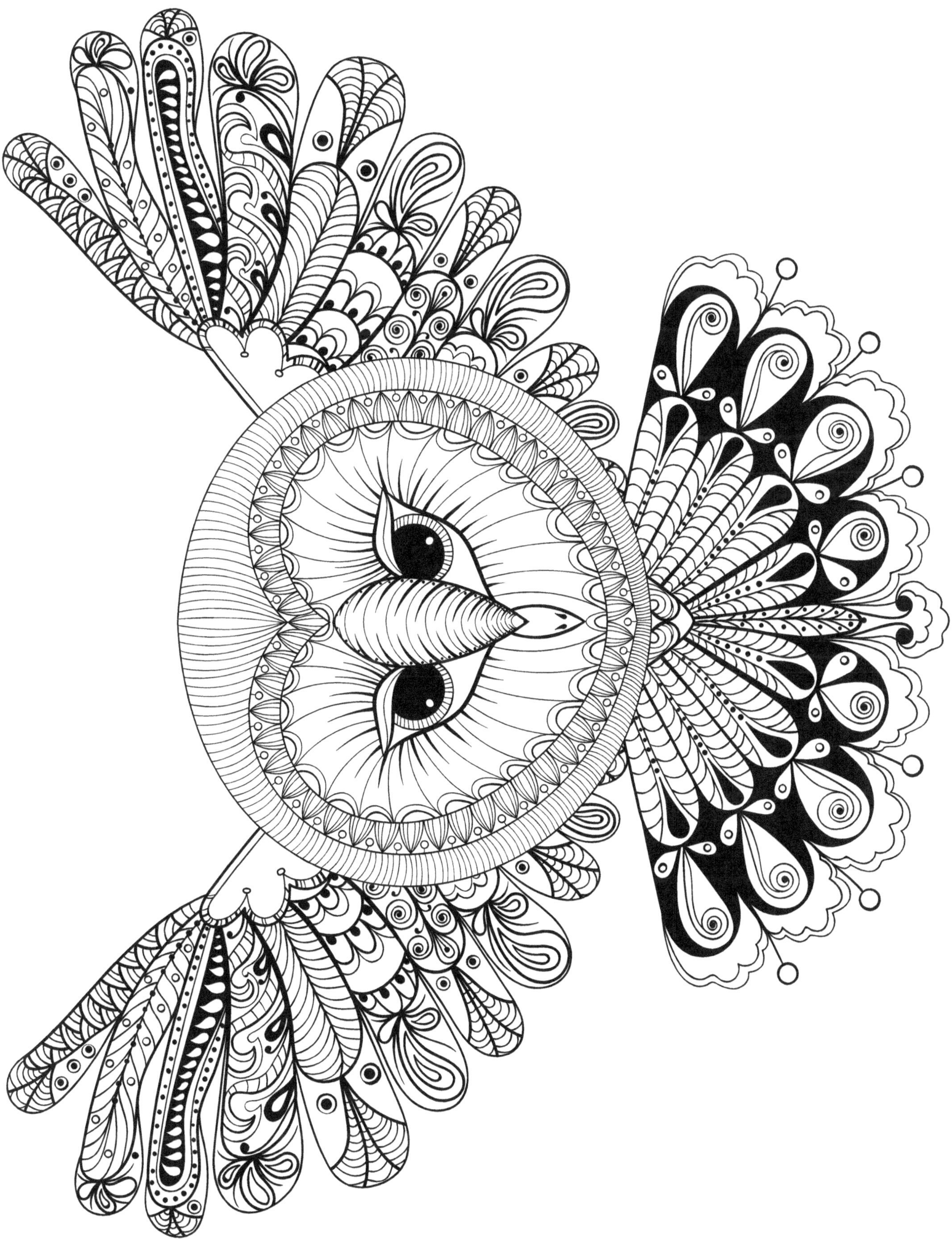

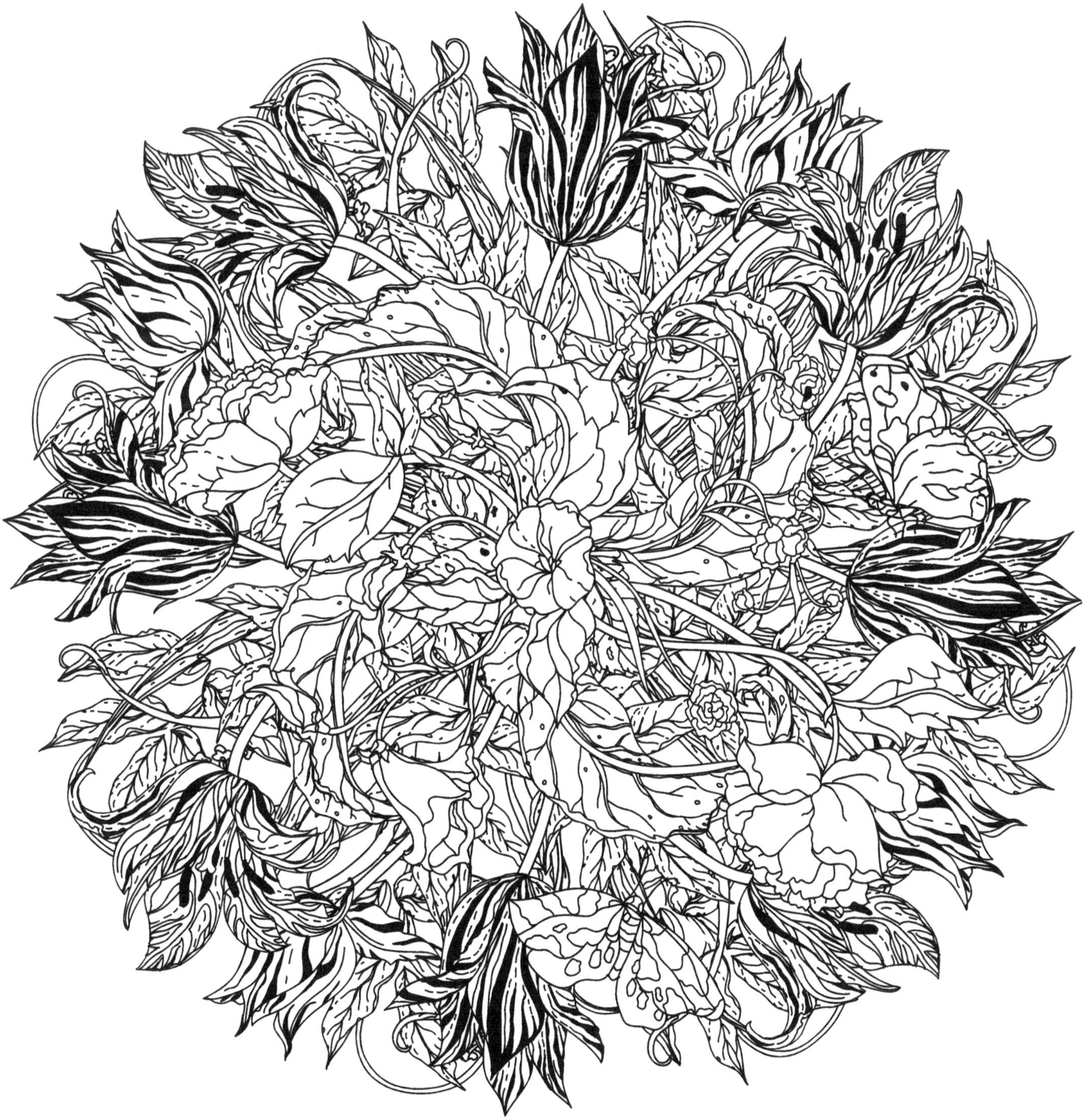

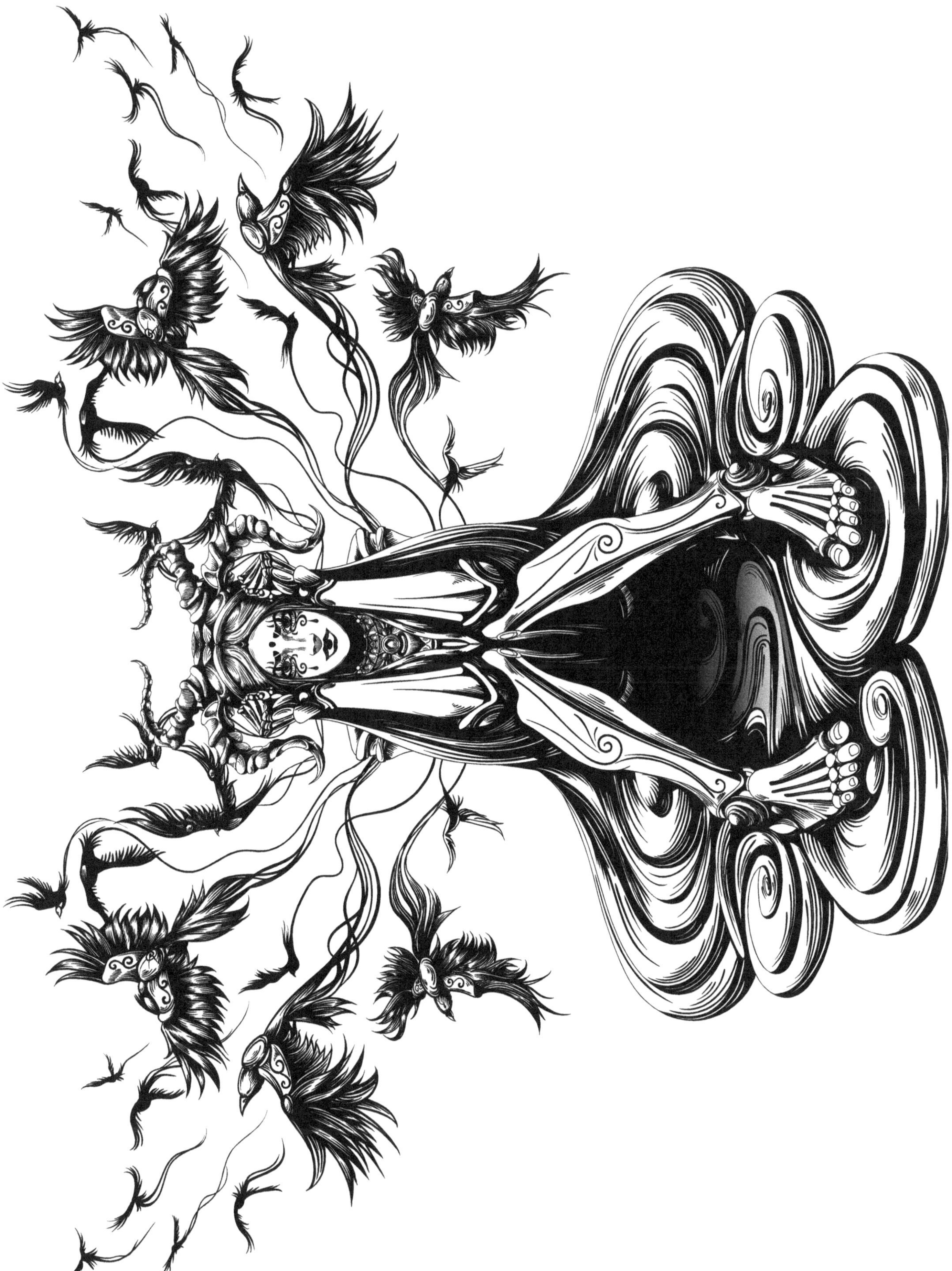

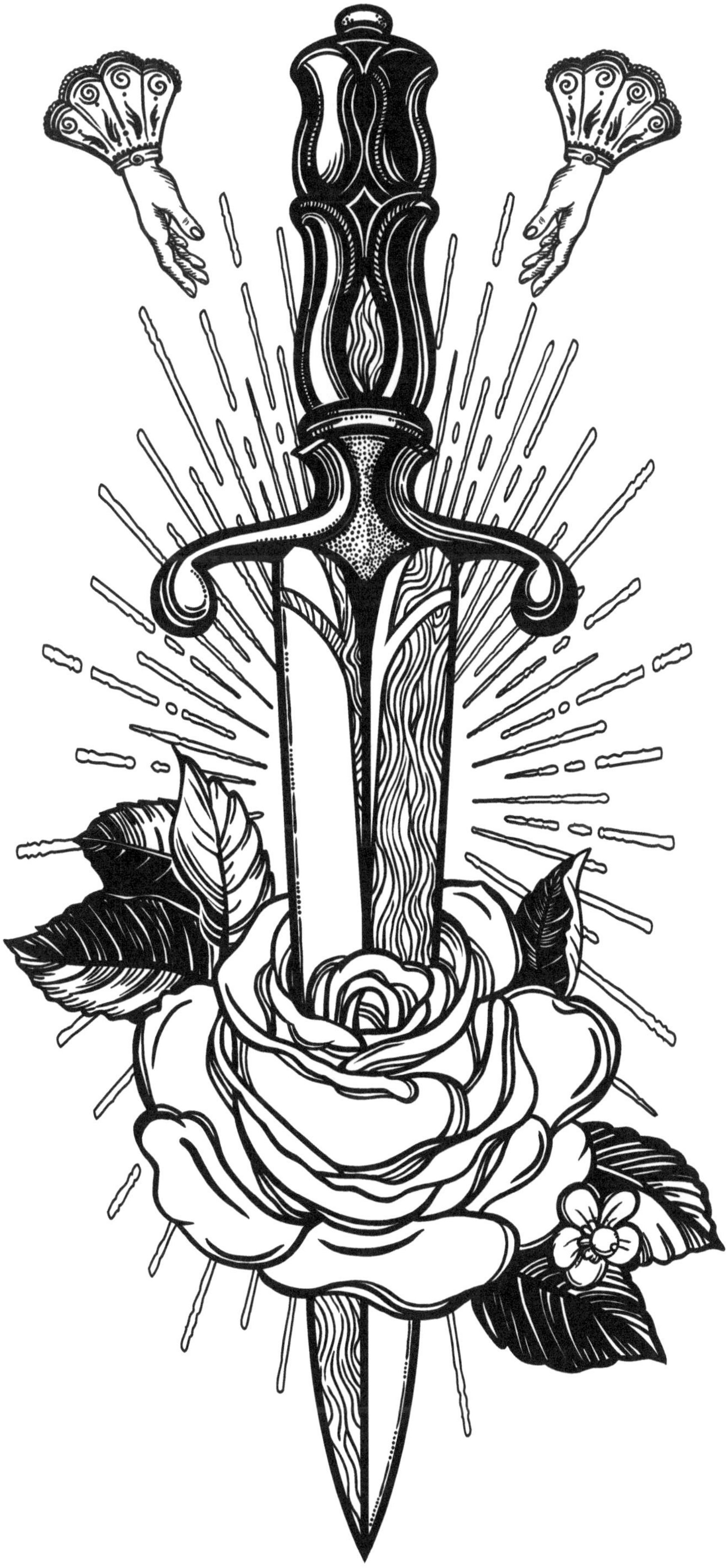

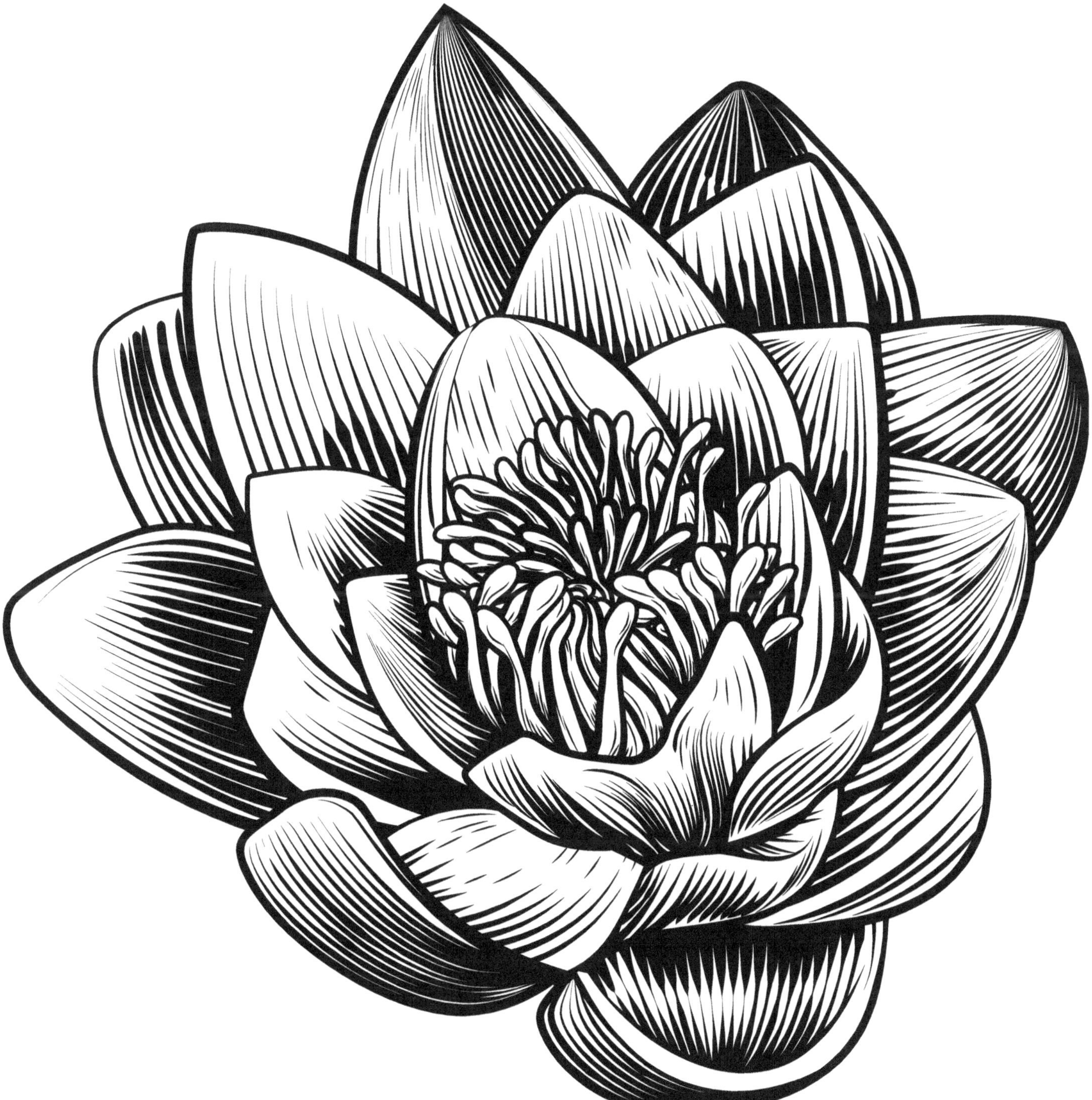

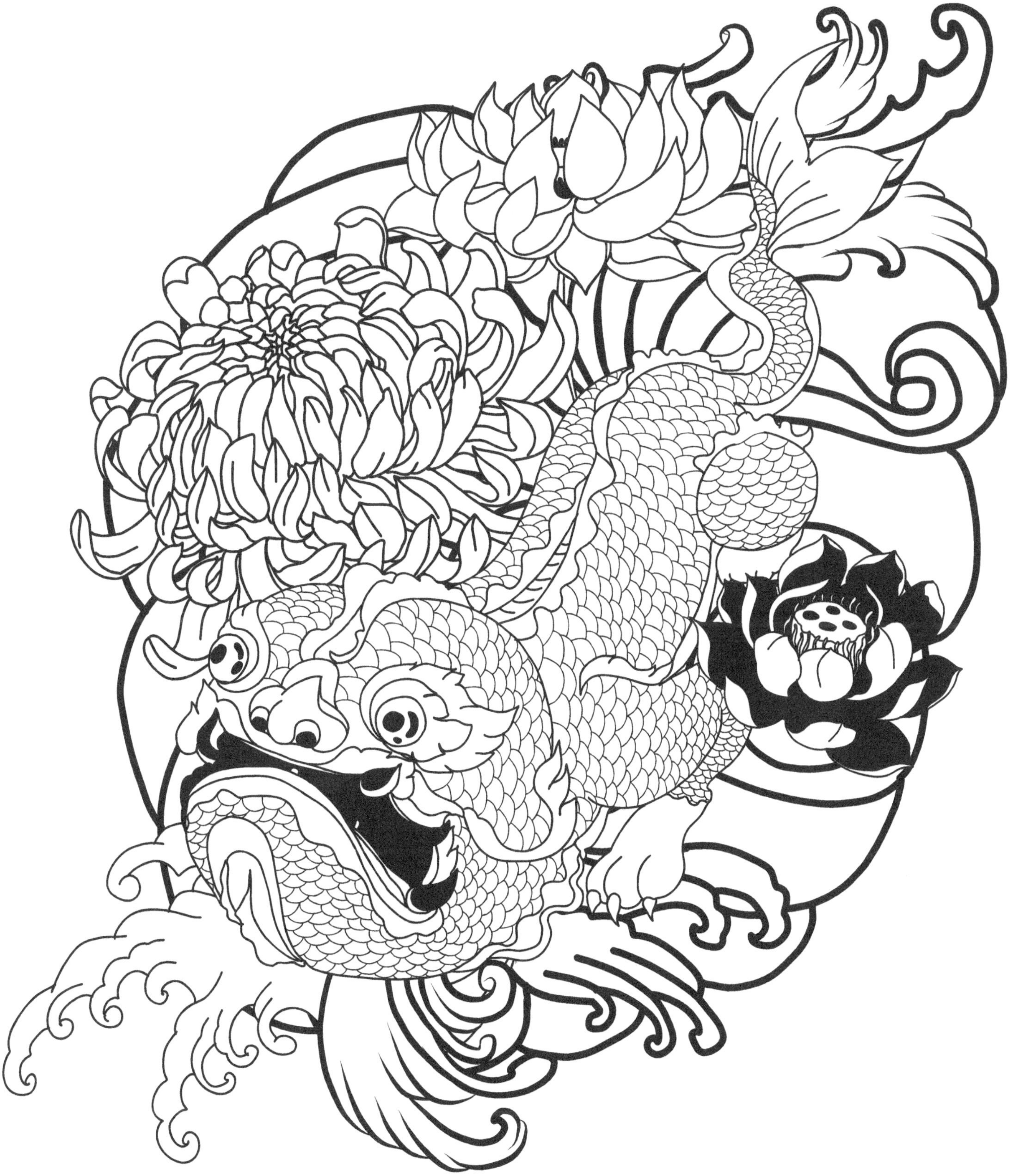

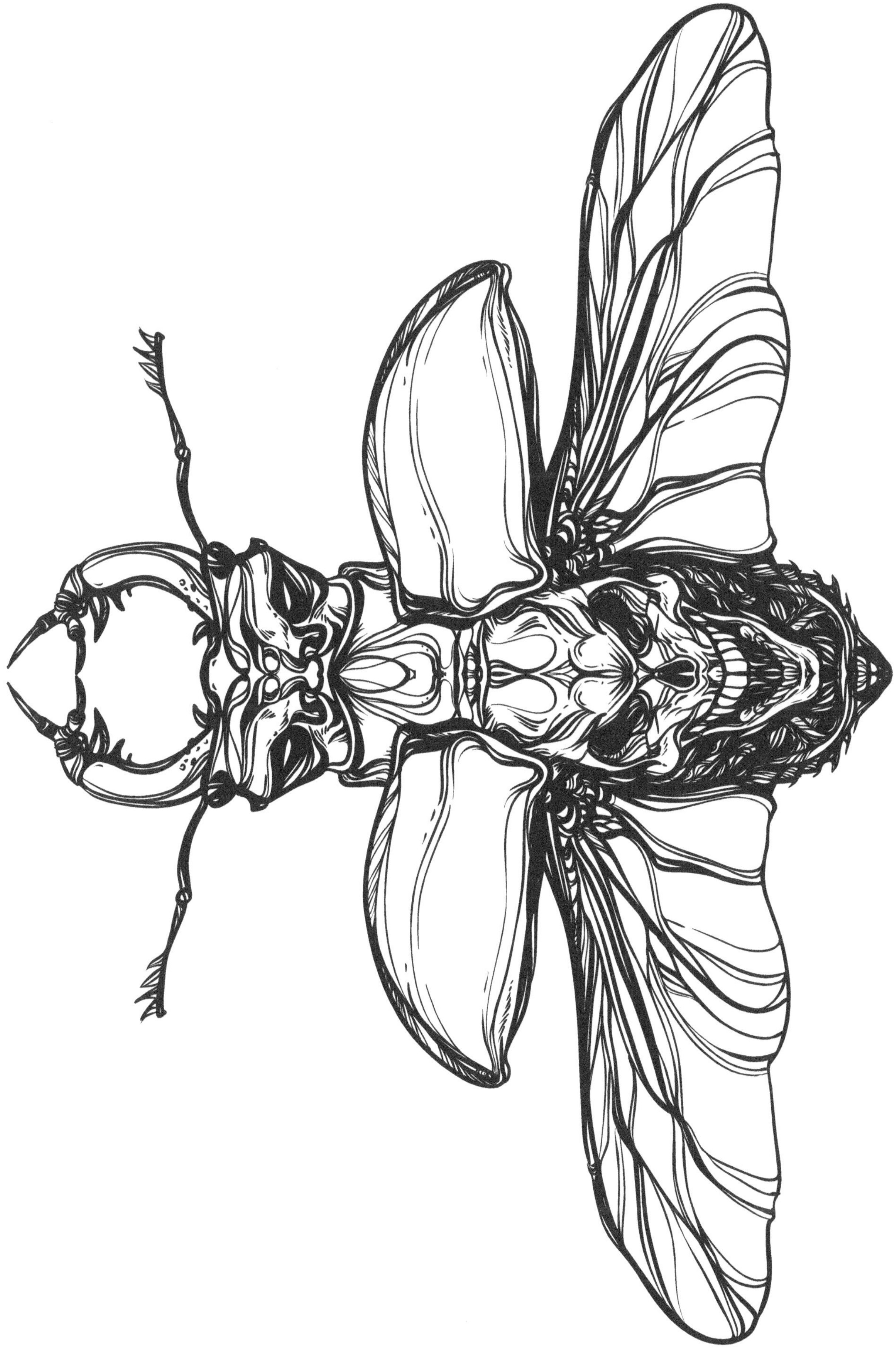

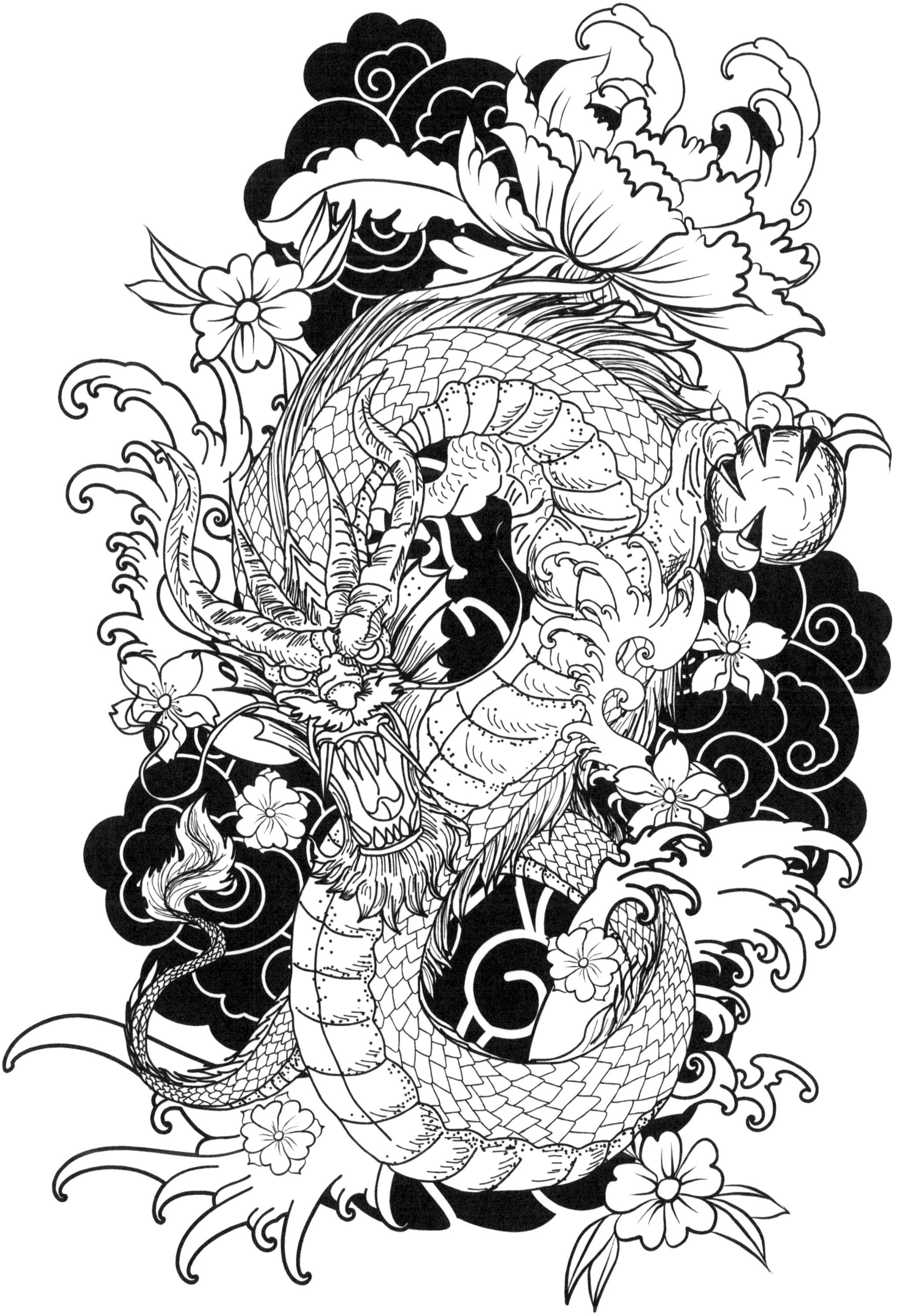

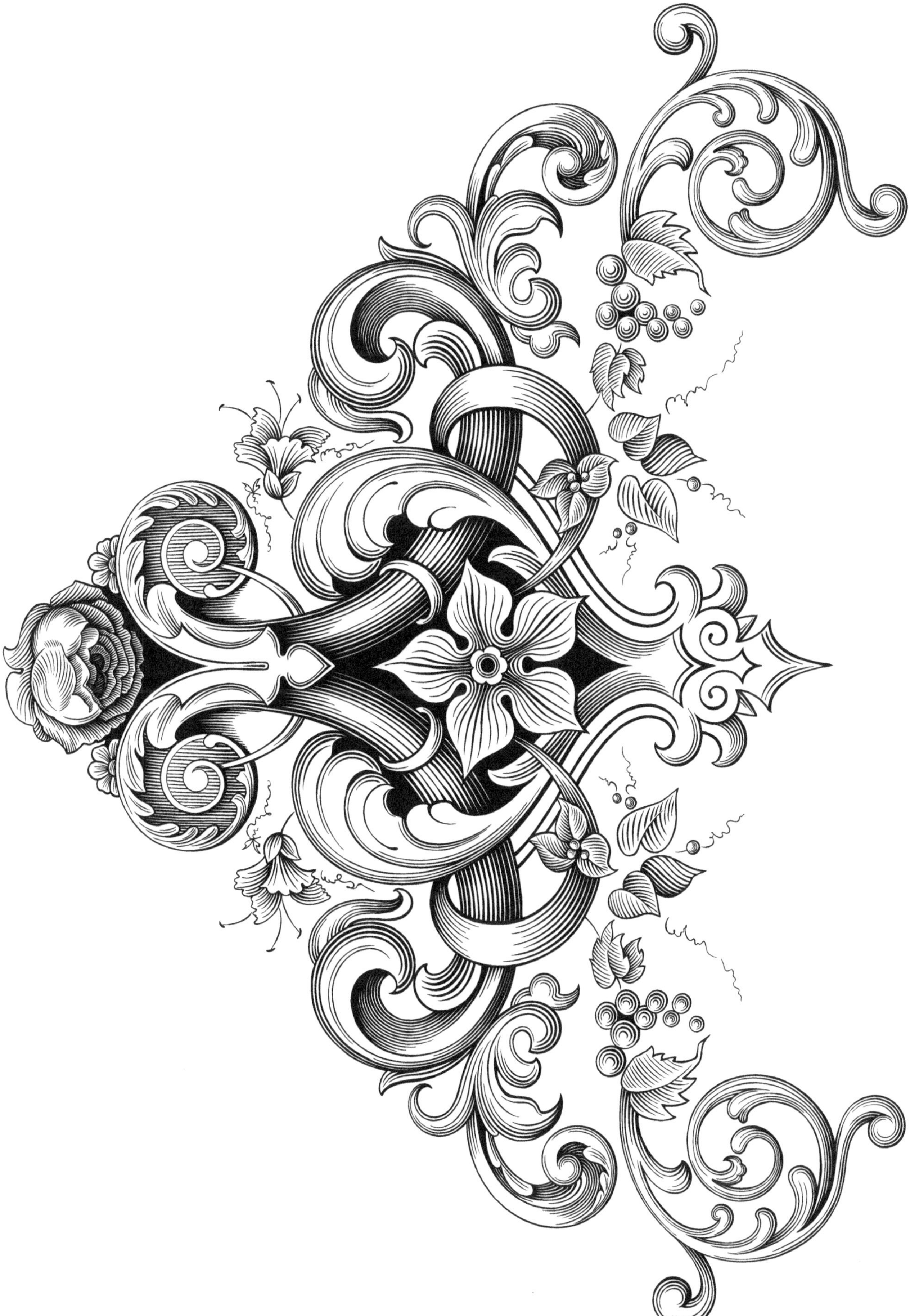

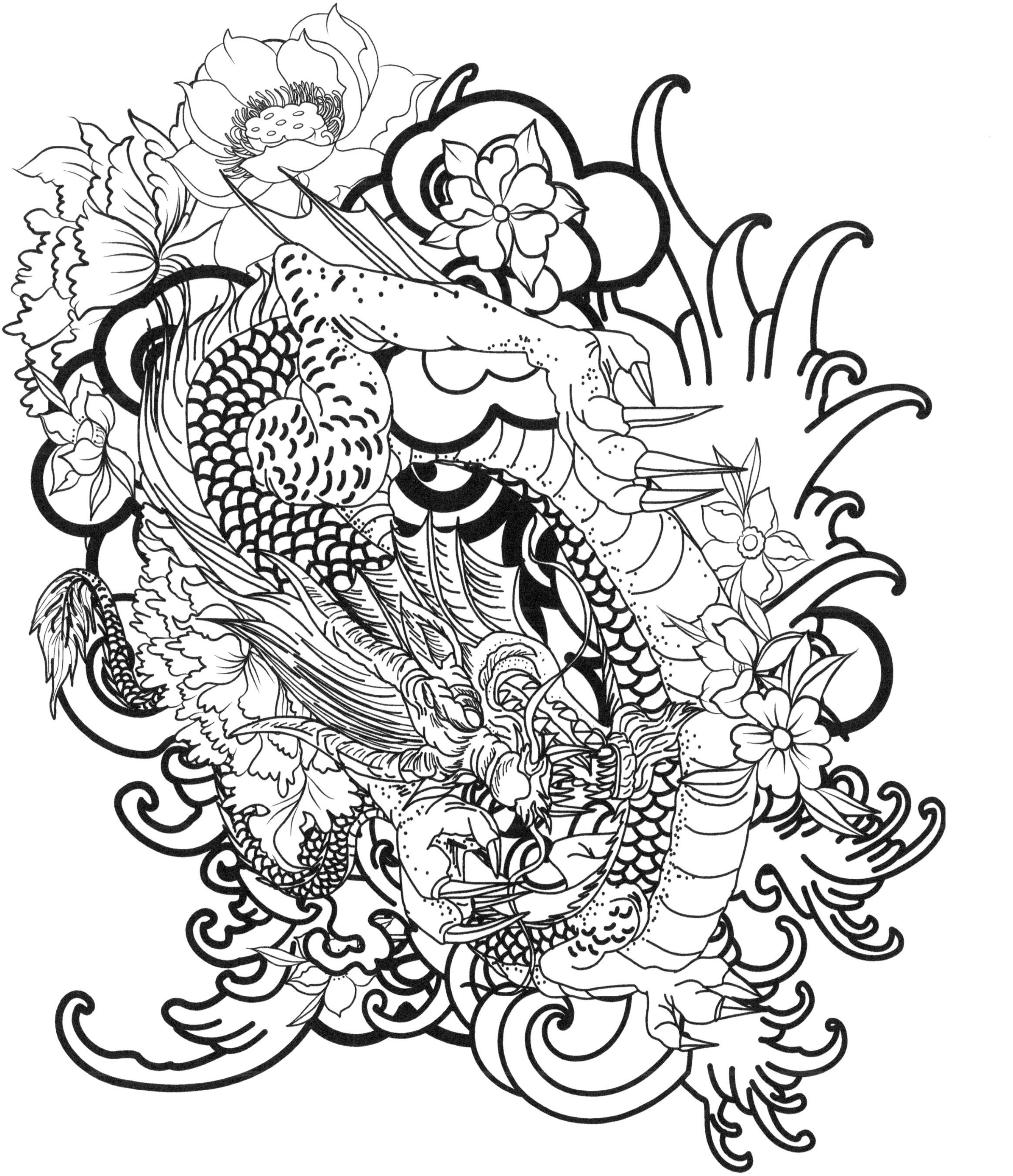

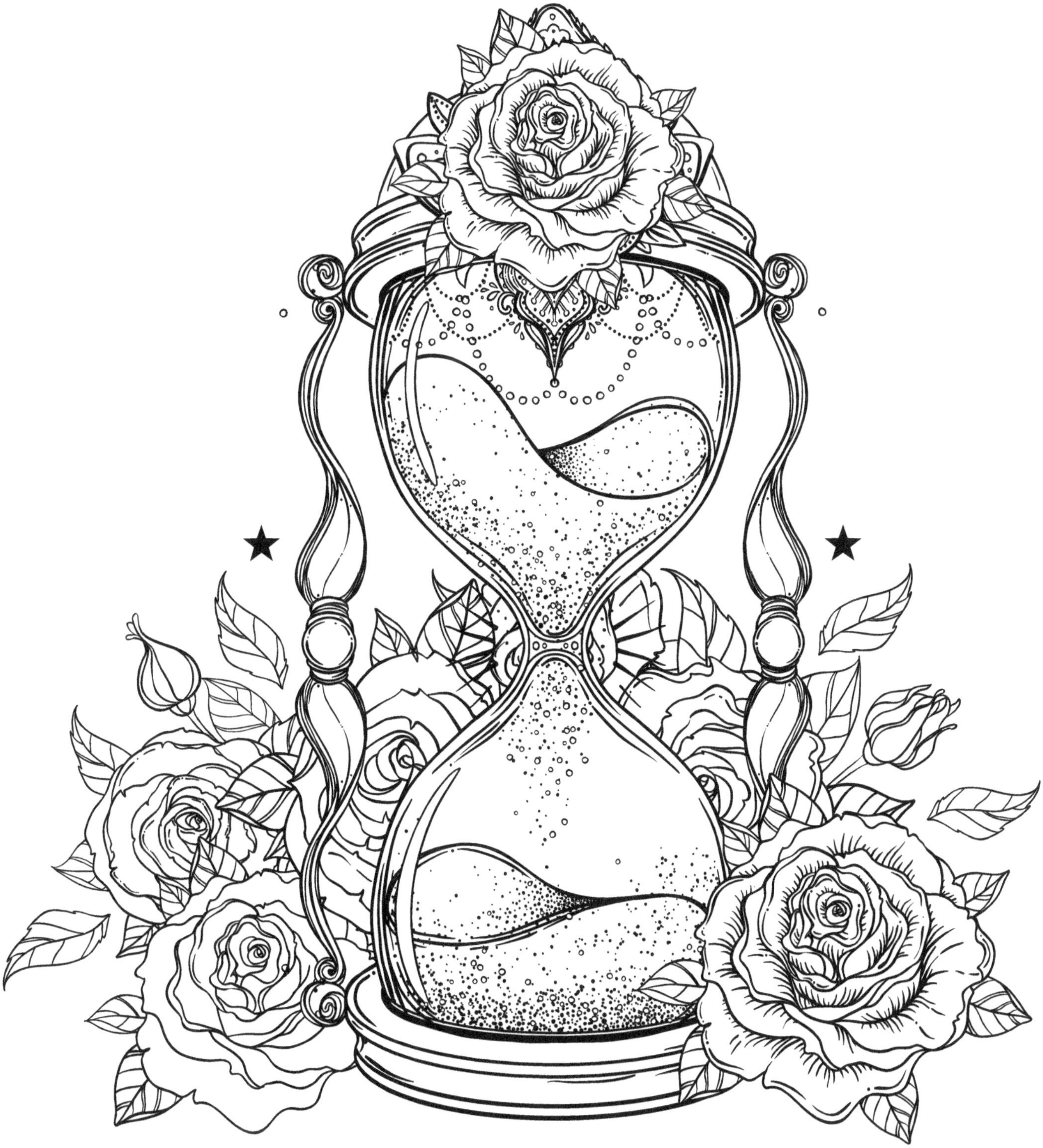

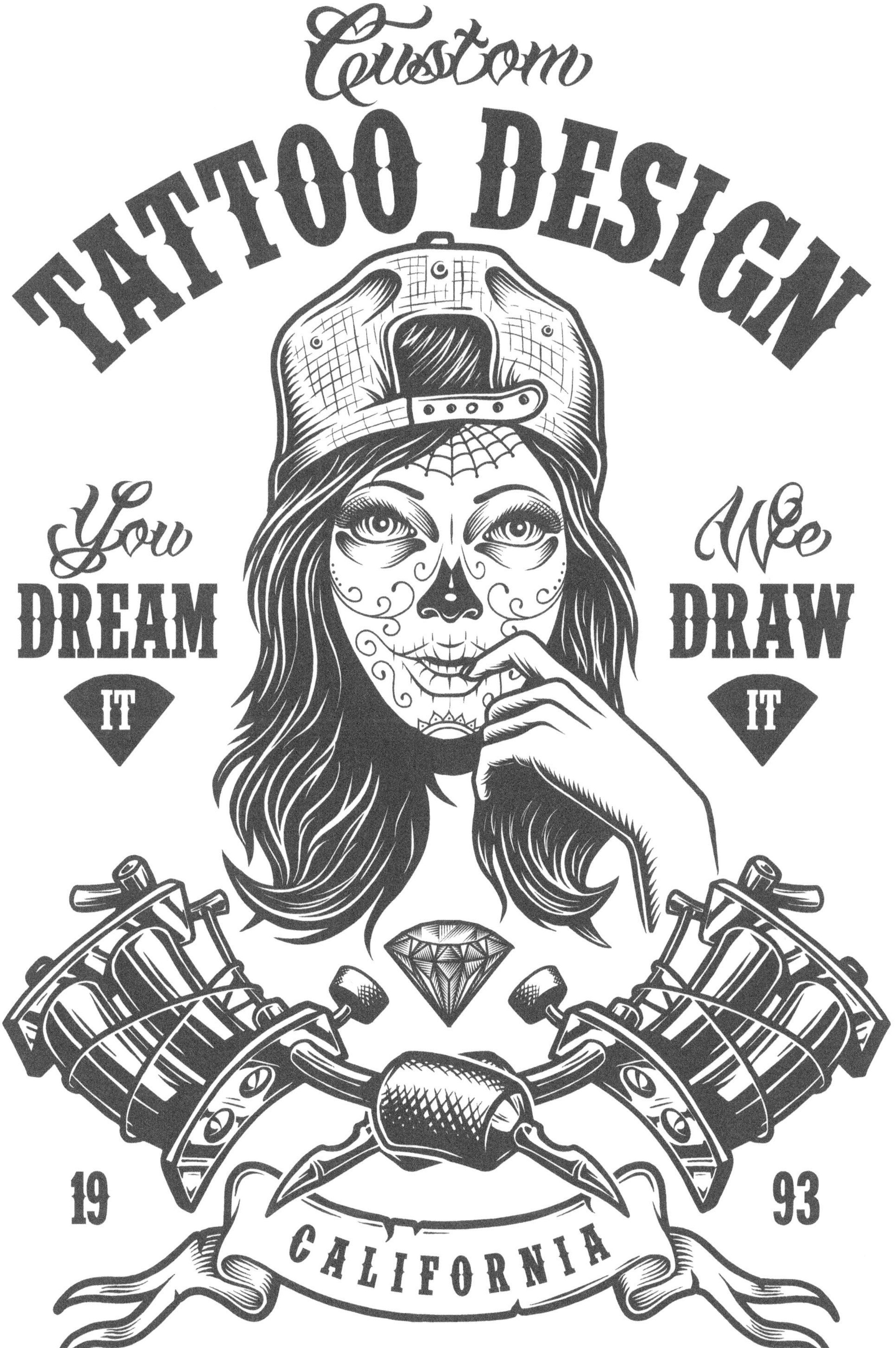
Custom
TATTOO DESIGN
You
DREAM
IT
We
DRAW
IT
19
93
CALIFORNIA

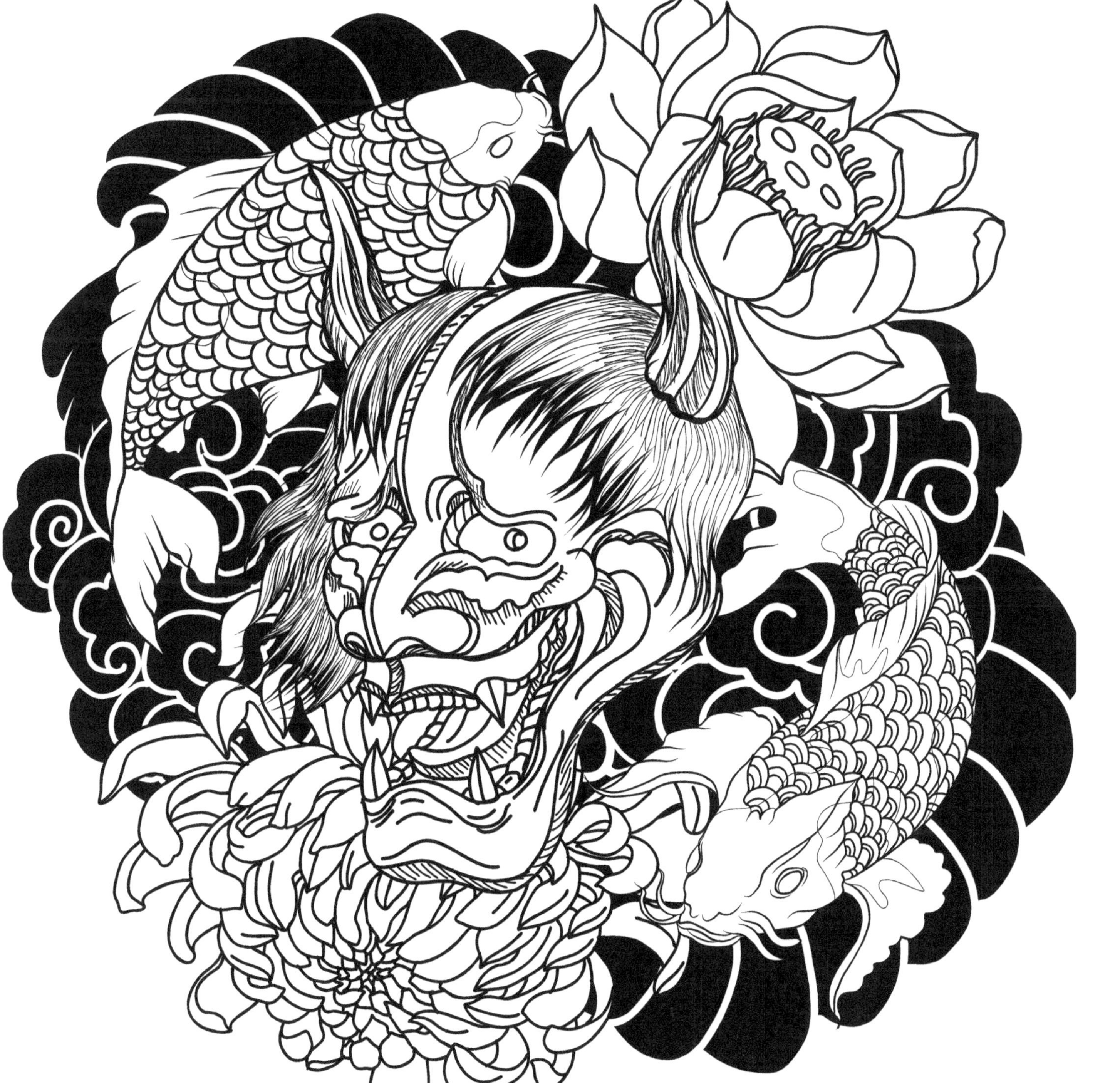

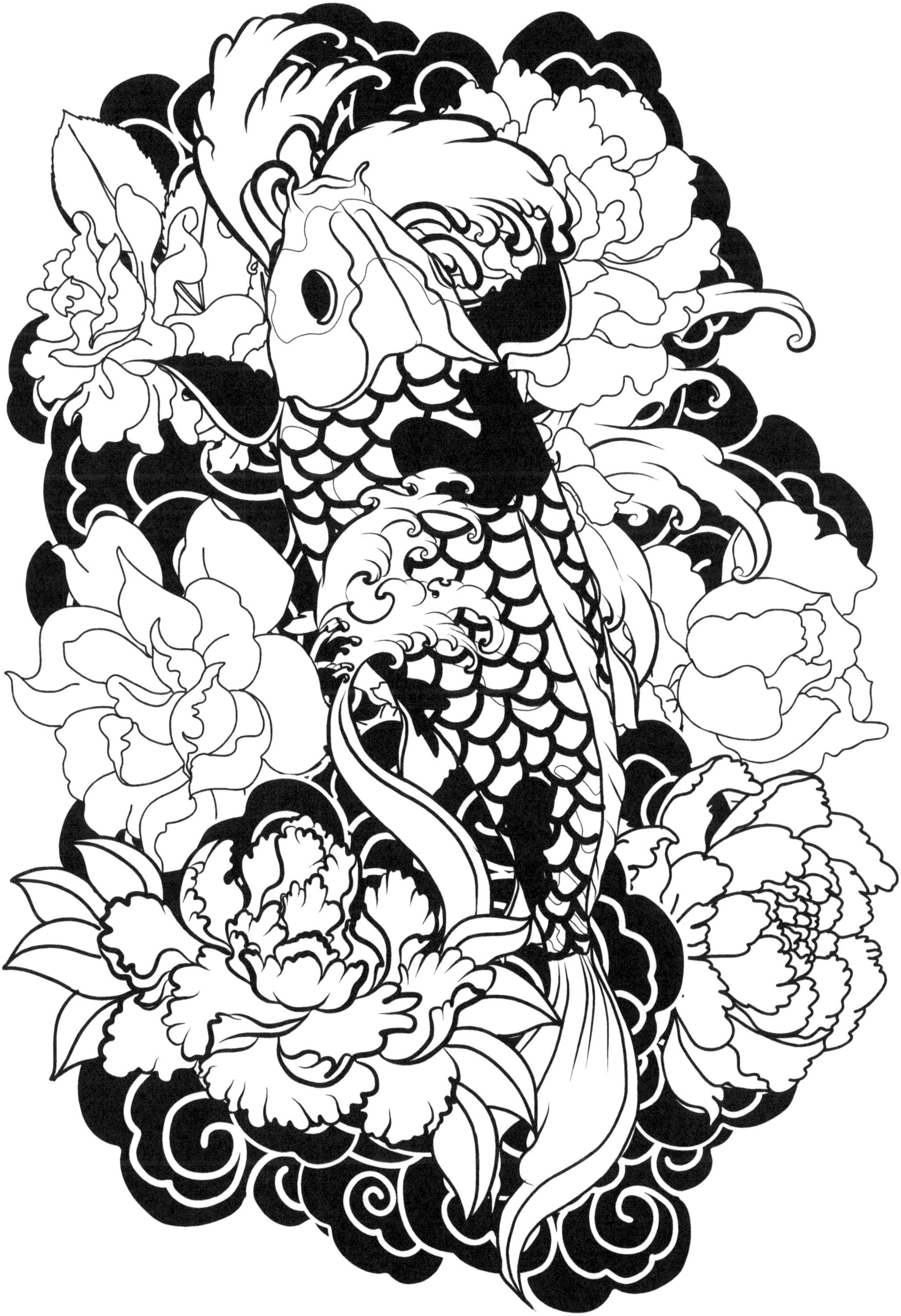

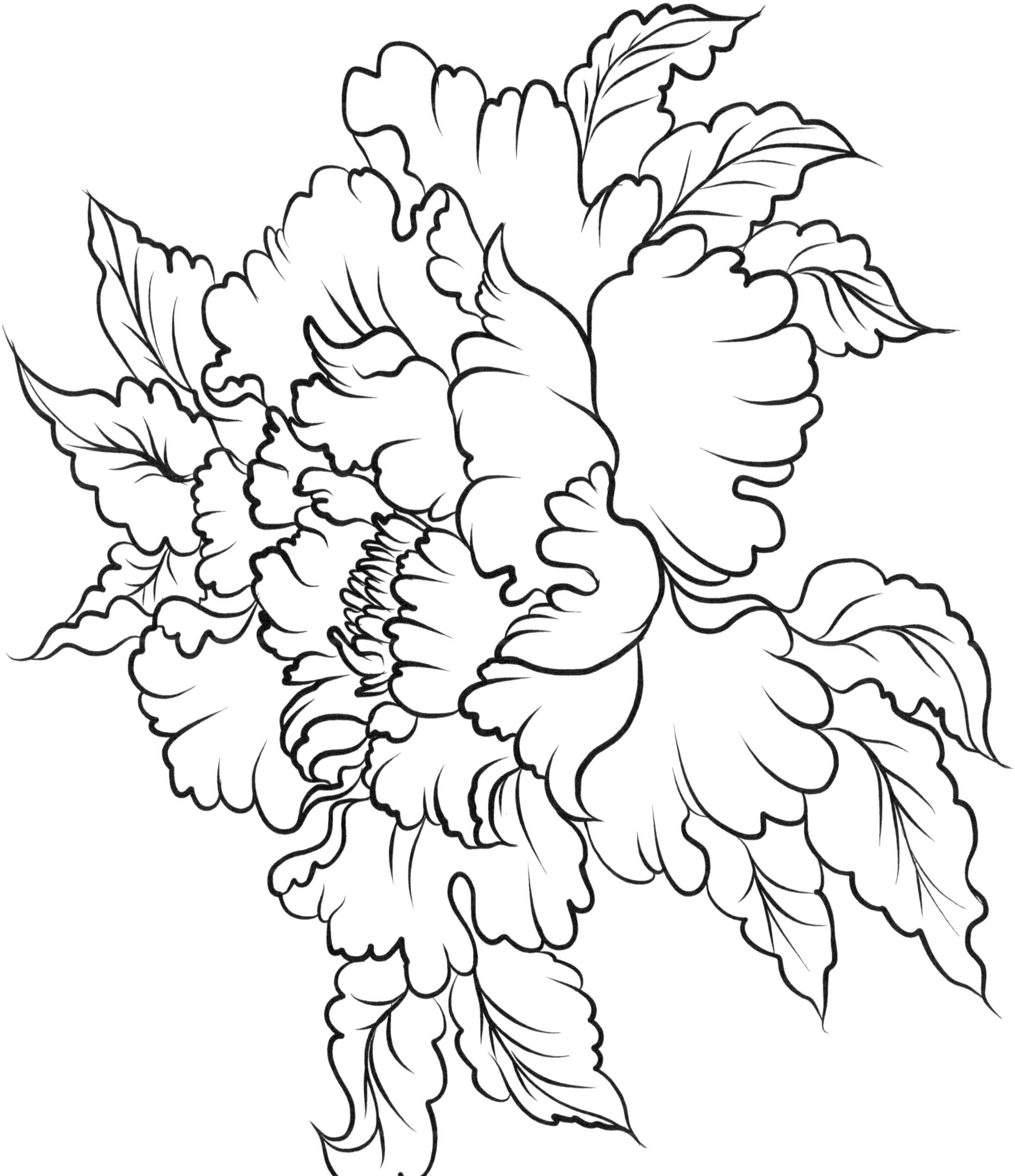

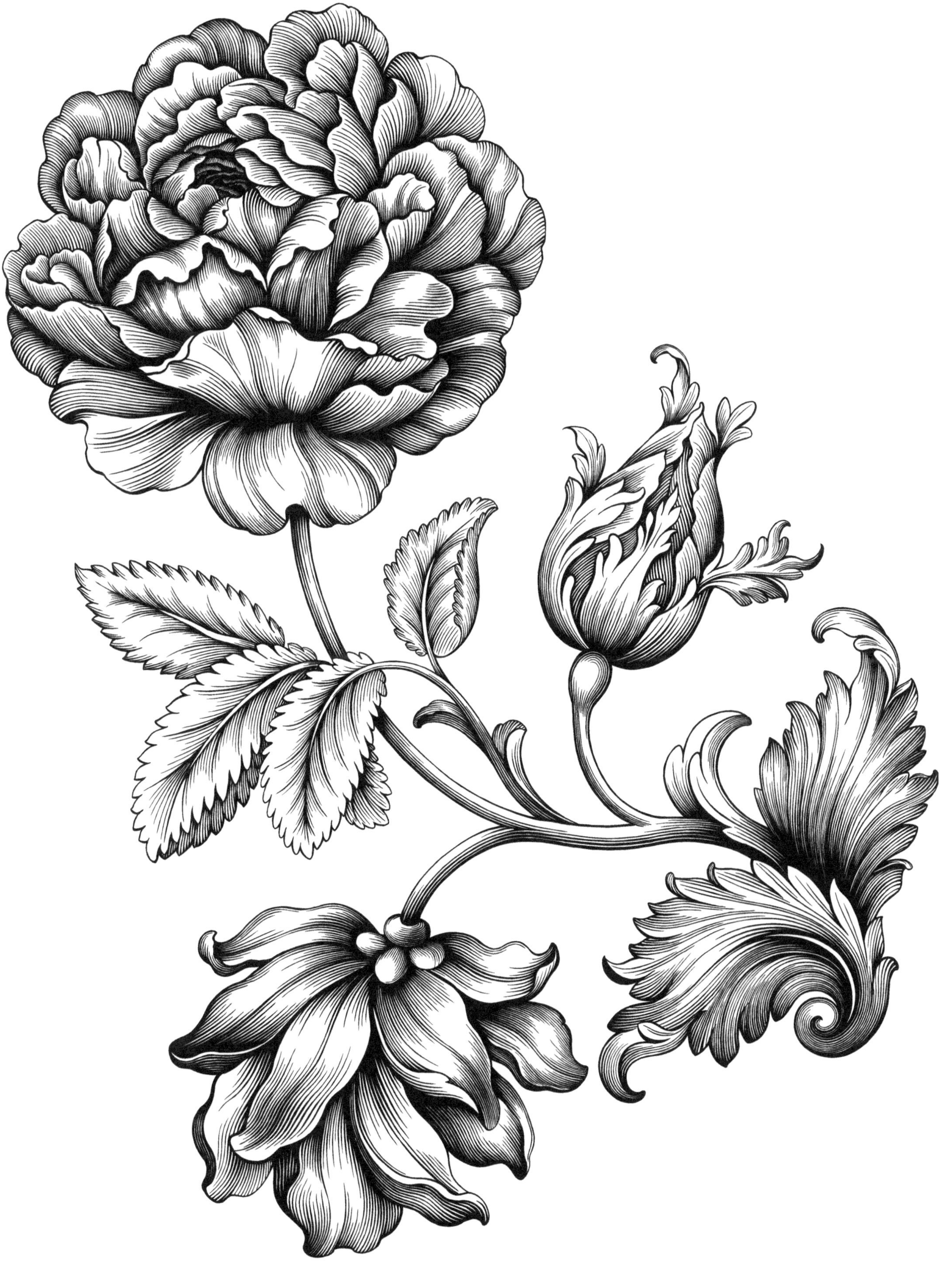

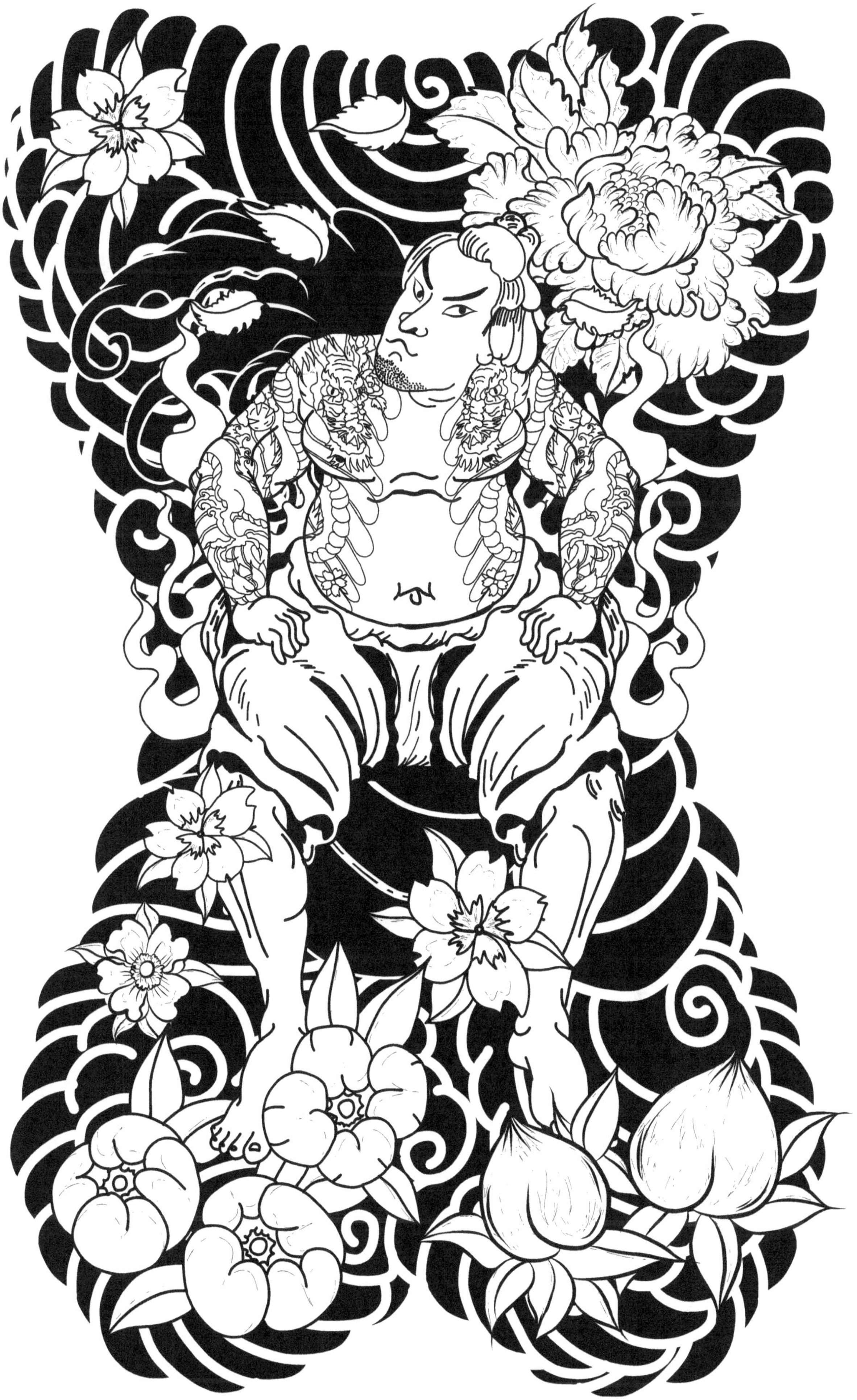

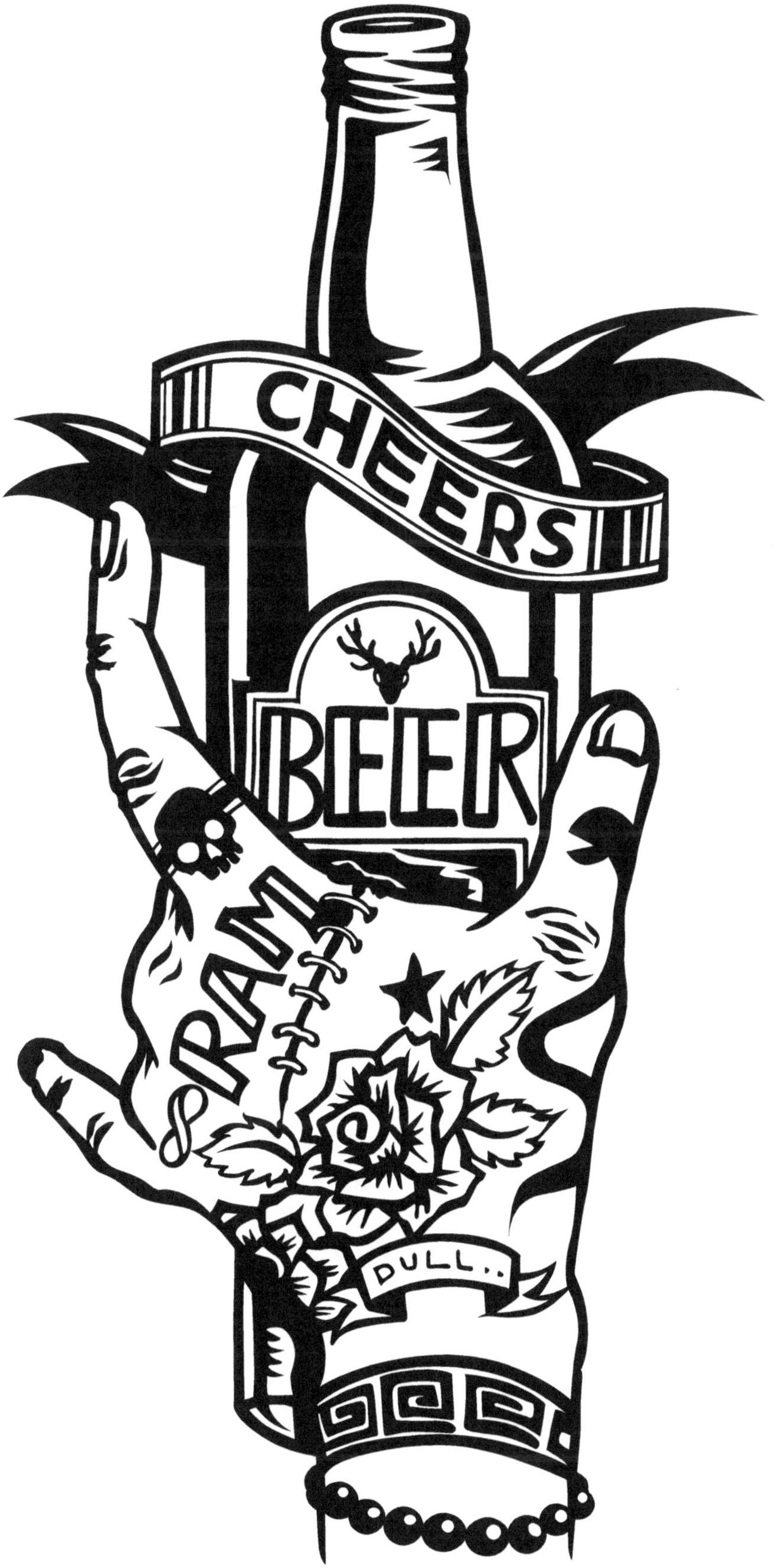
CHEERS
BEER
RAM
DULL..

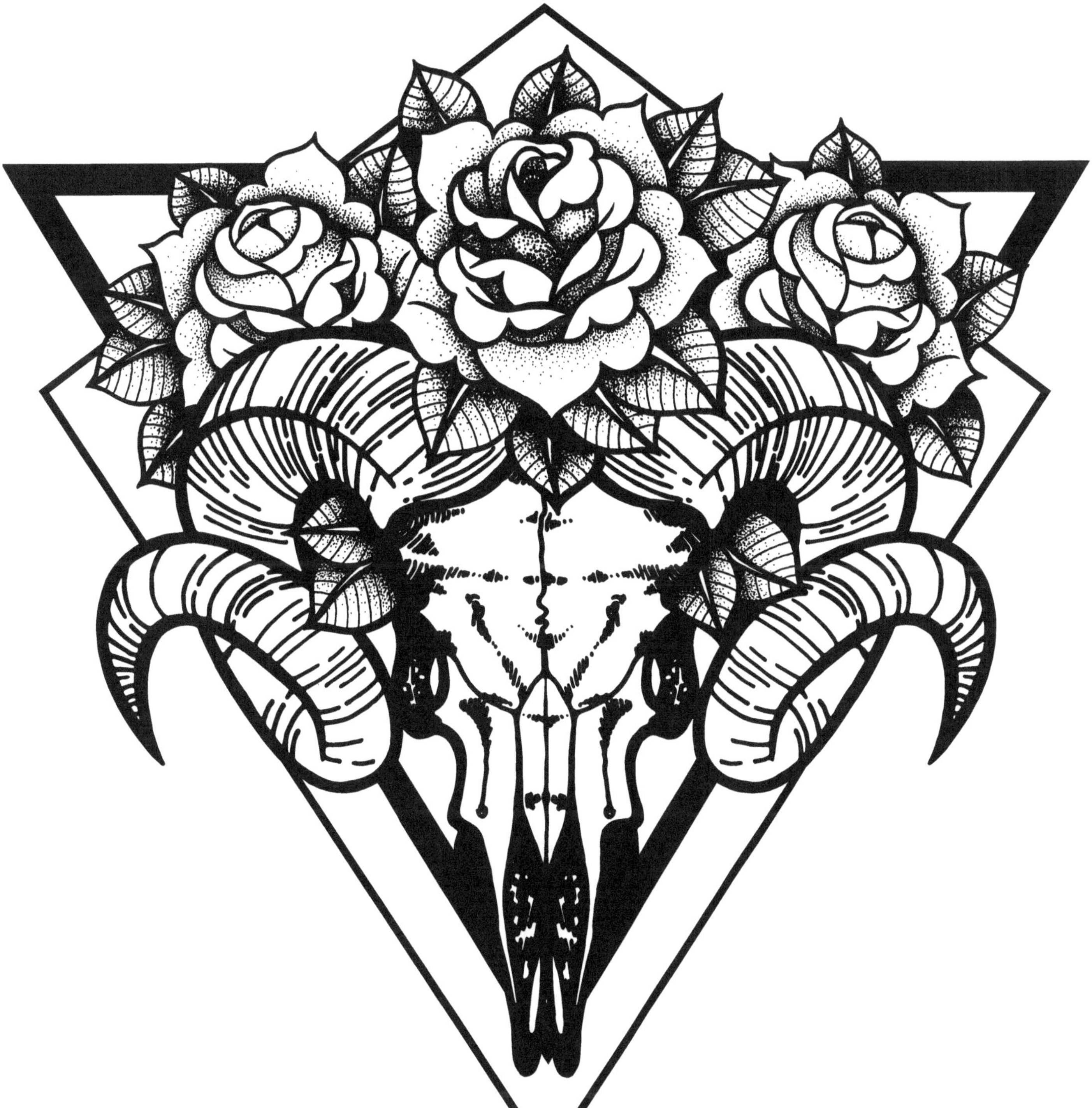

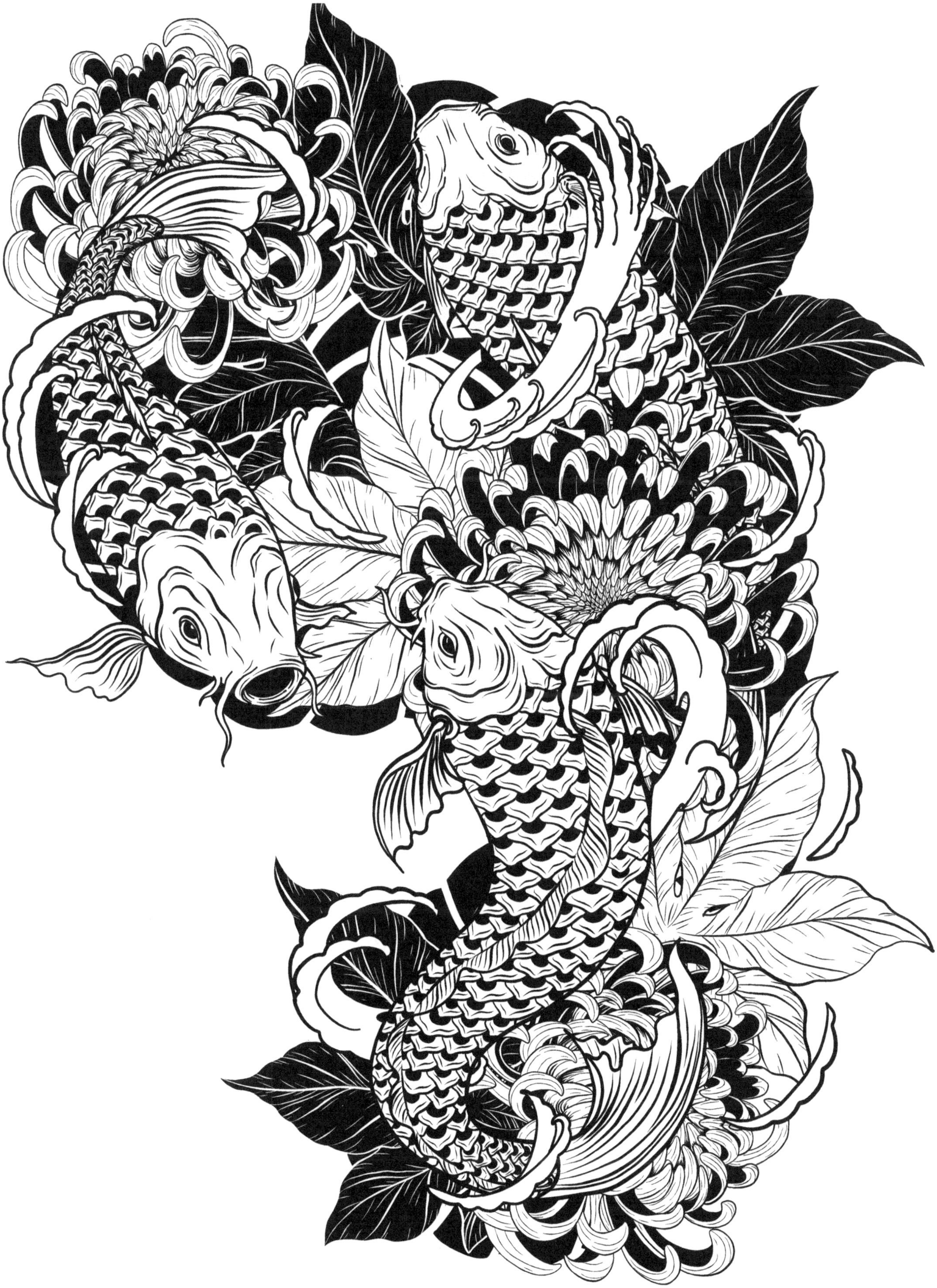

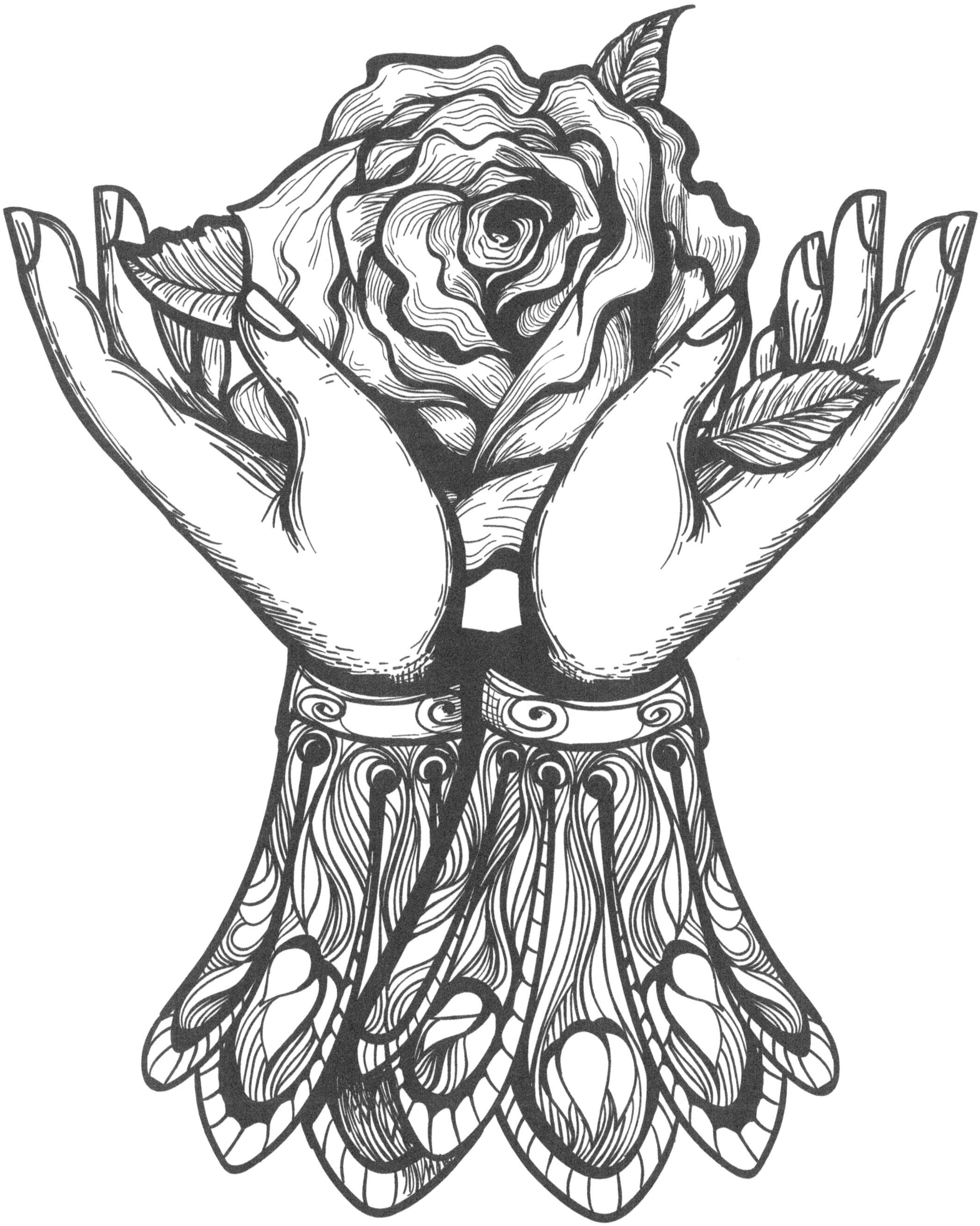

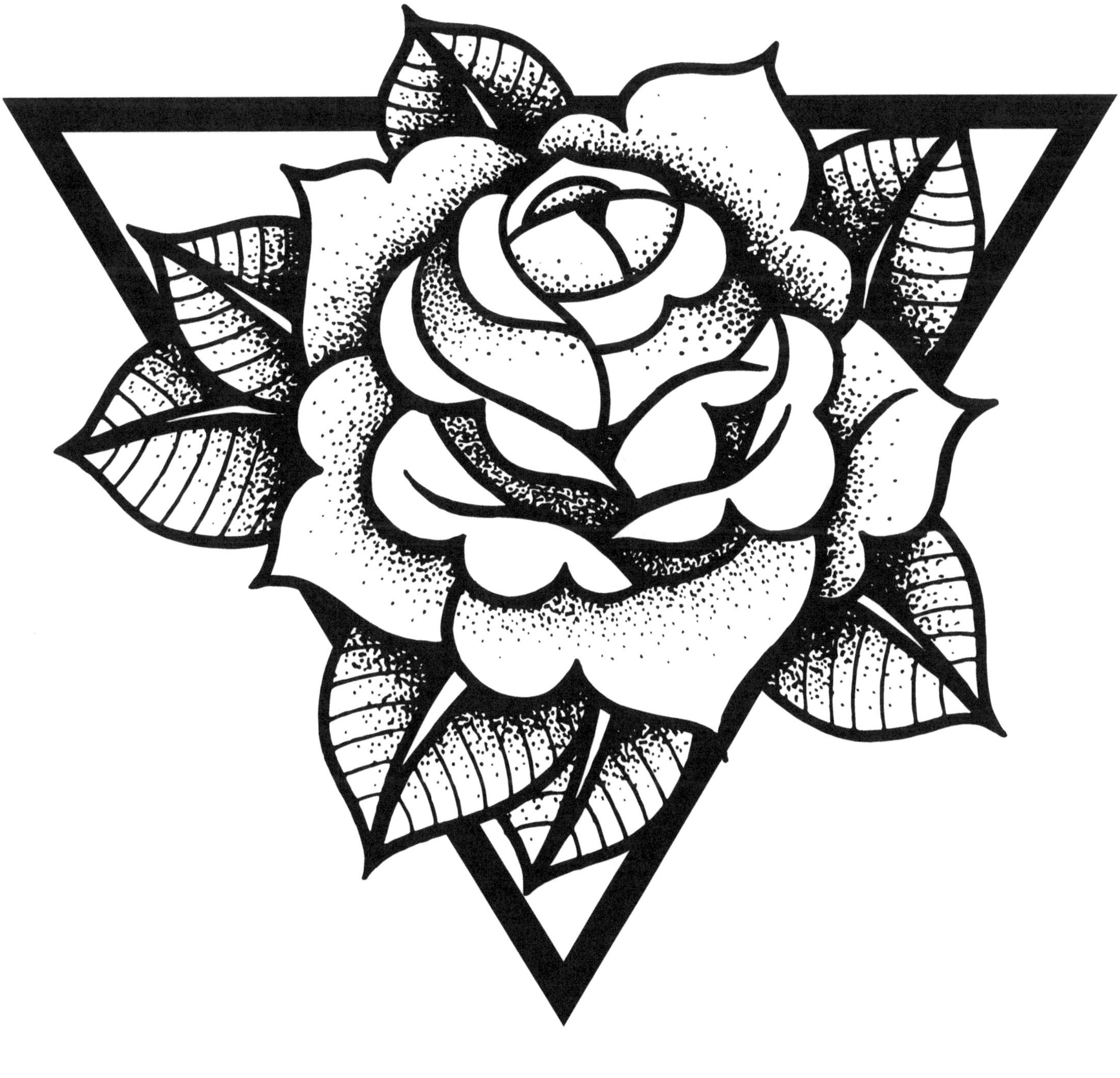

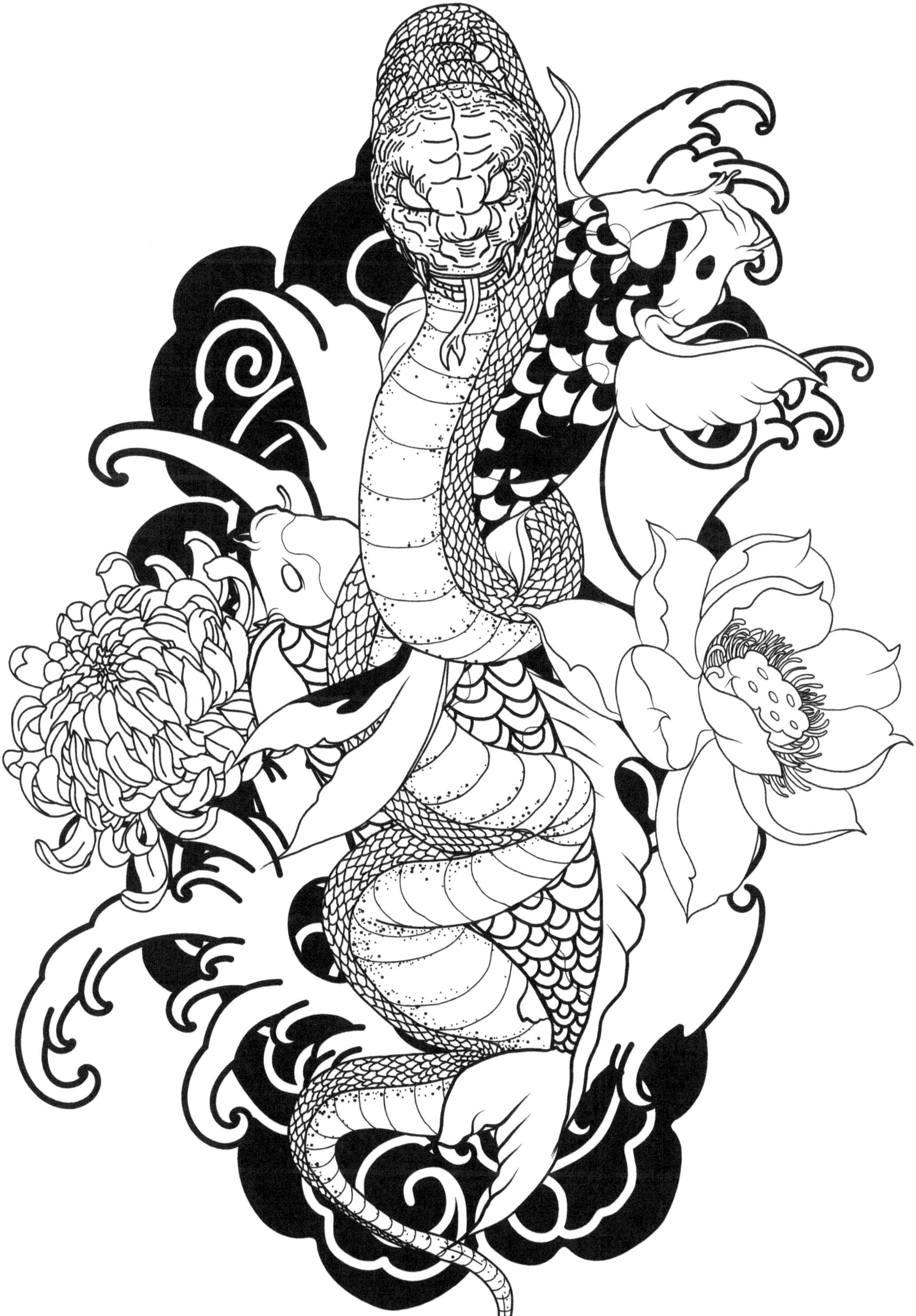

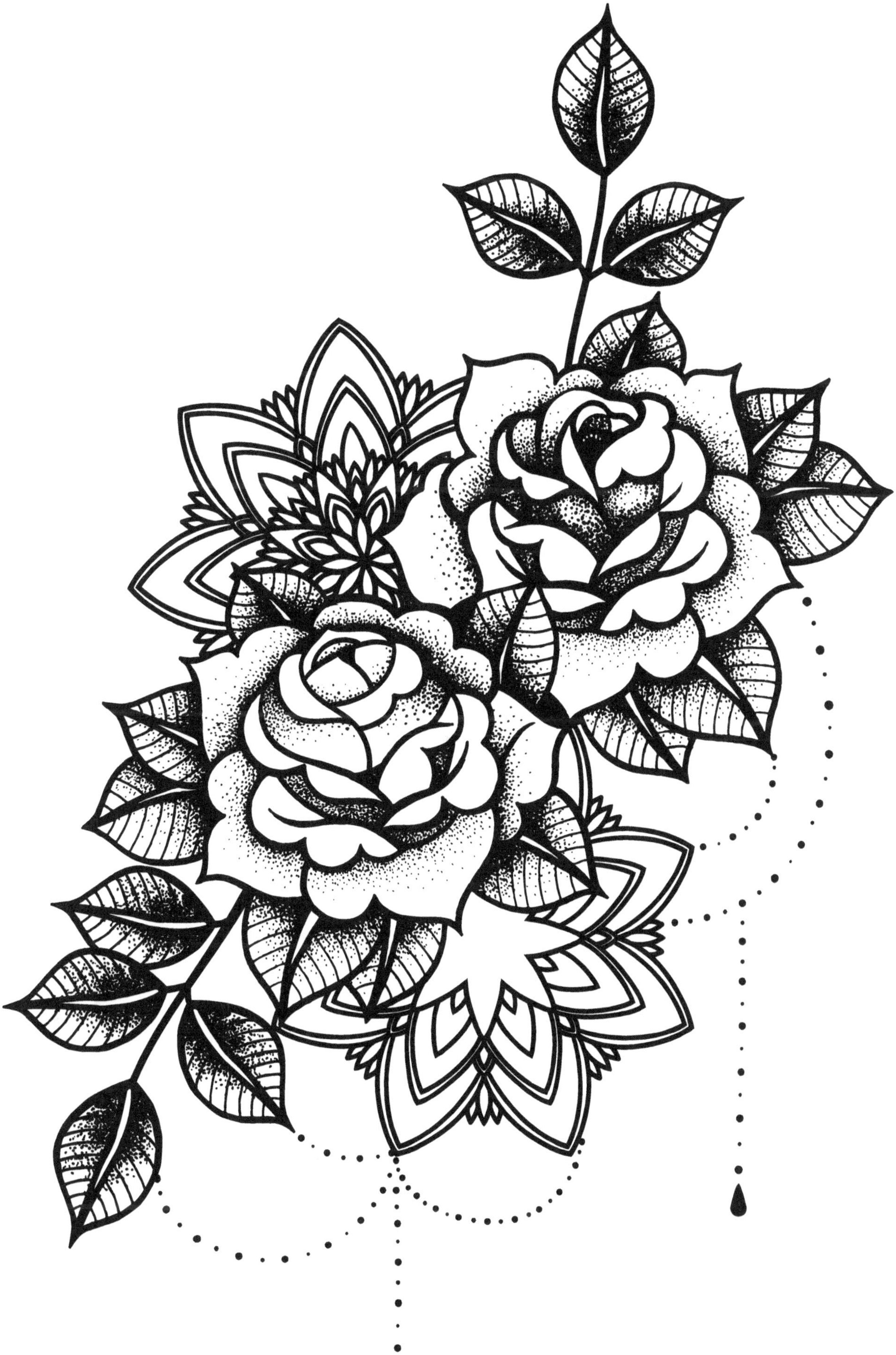

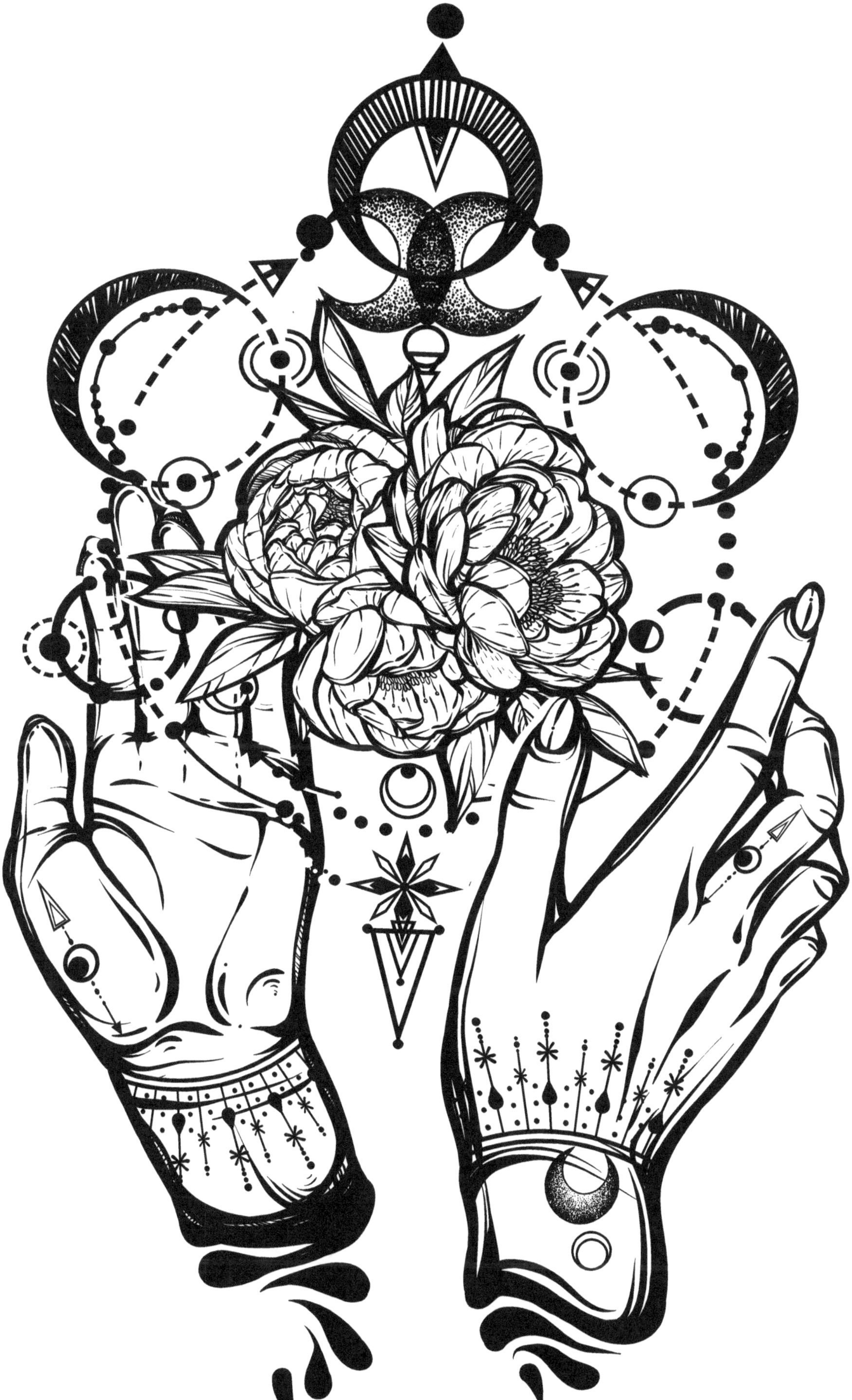

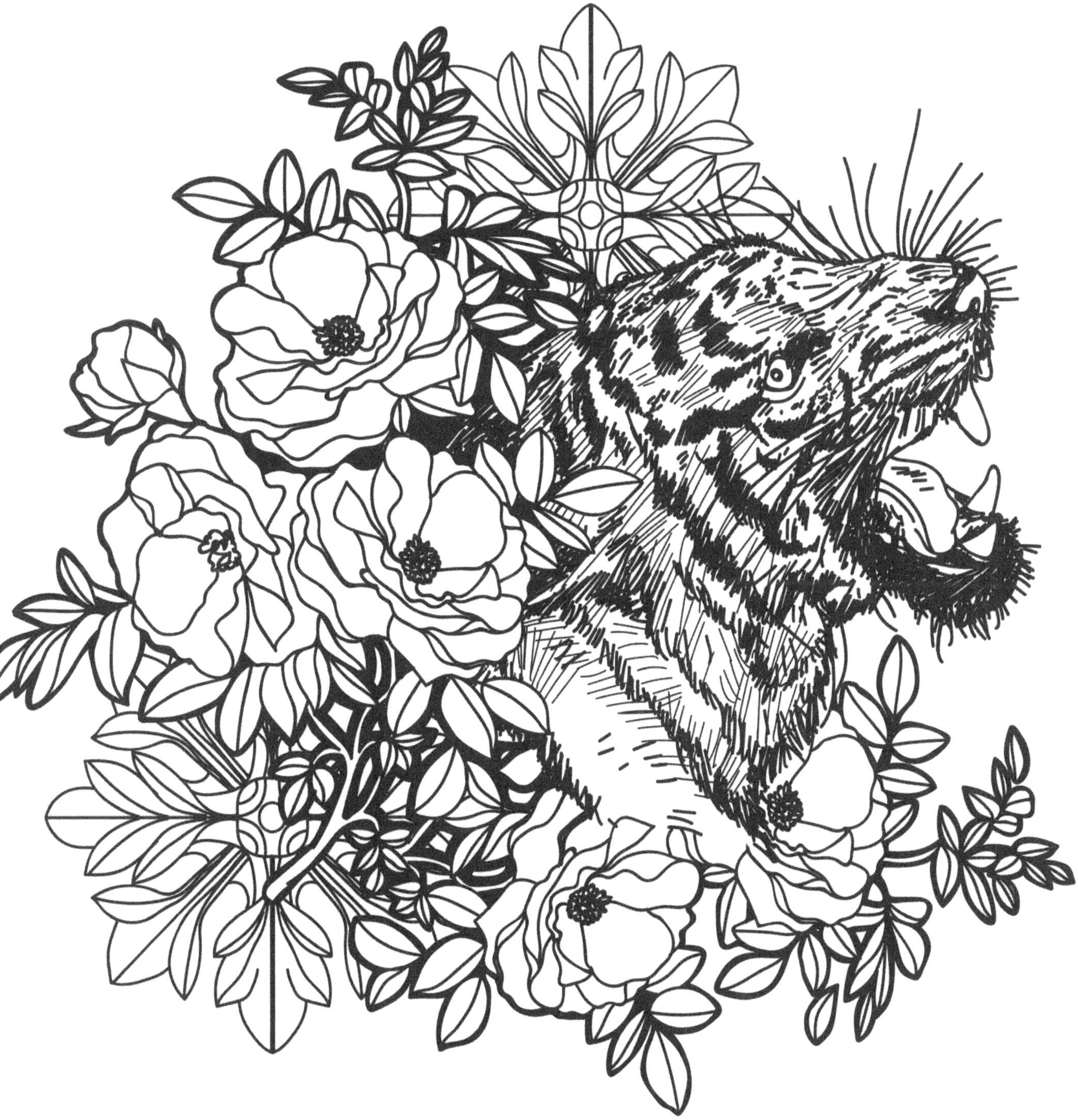

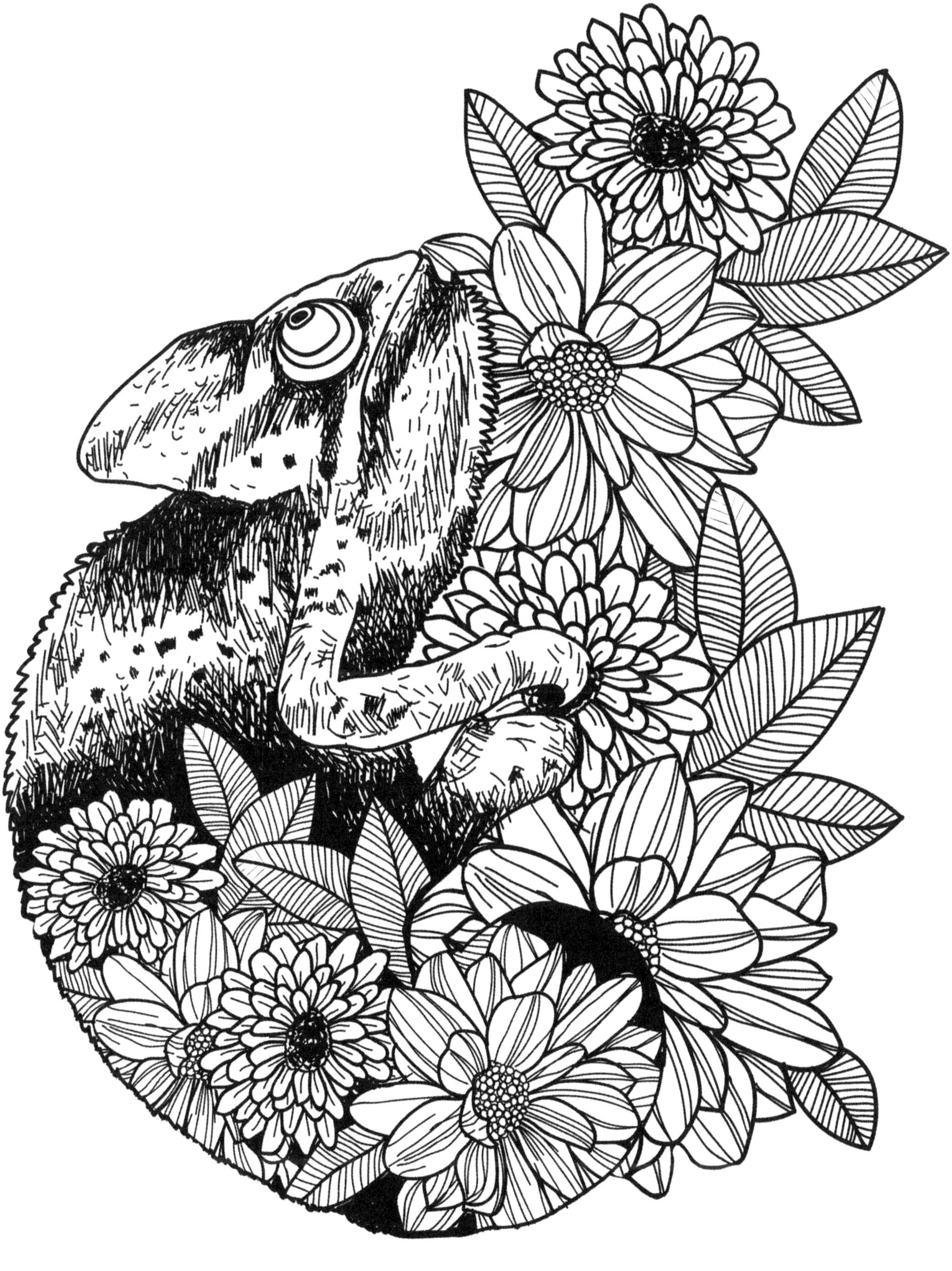

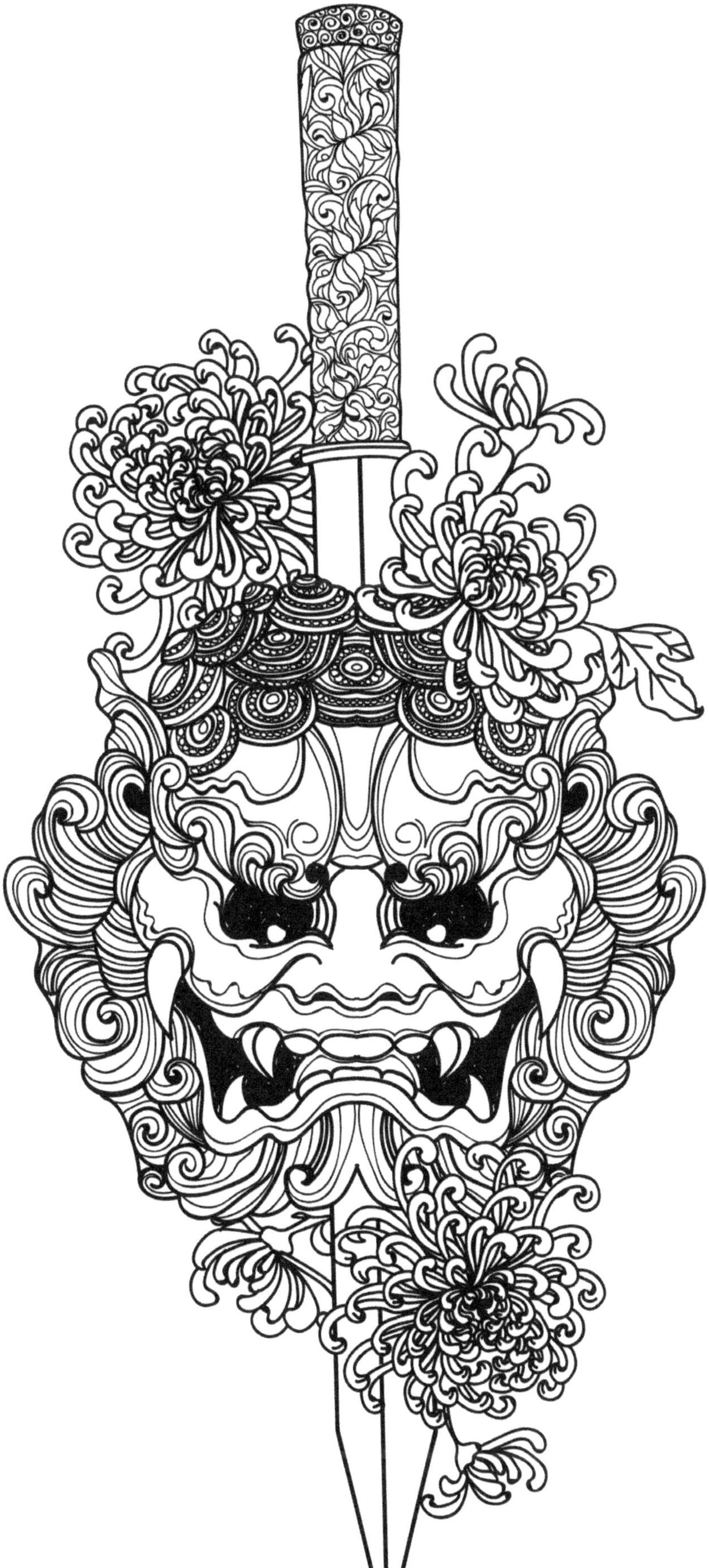

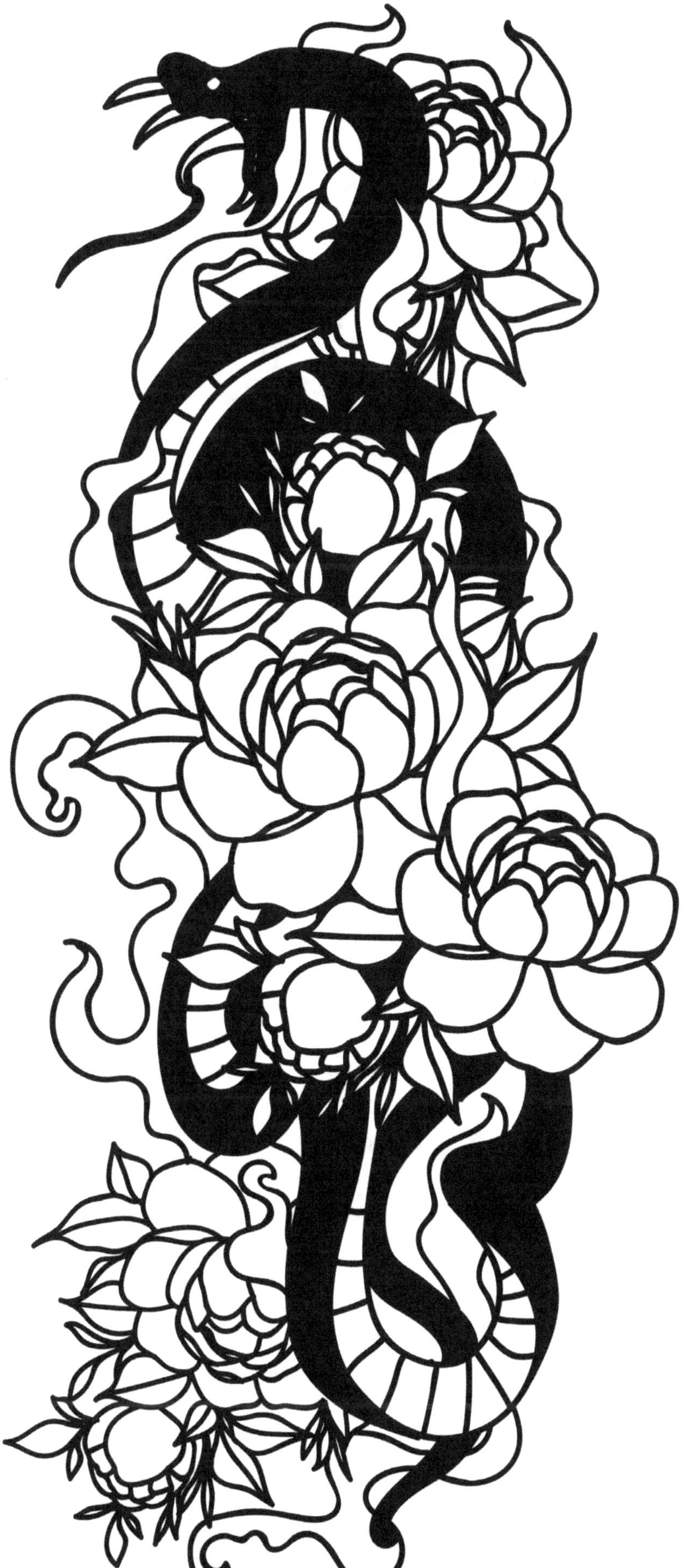

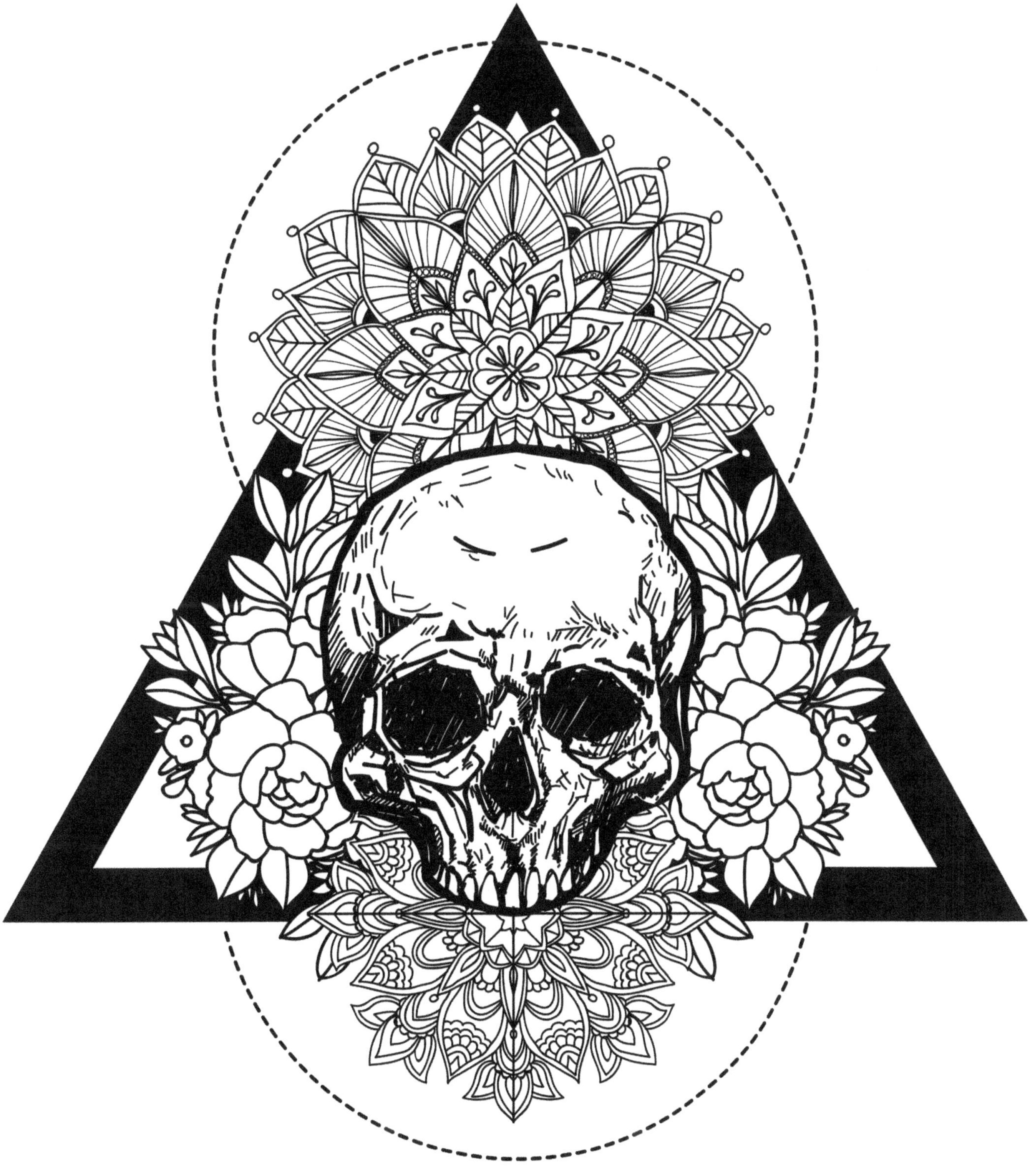

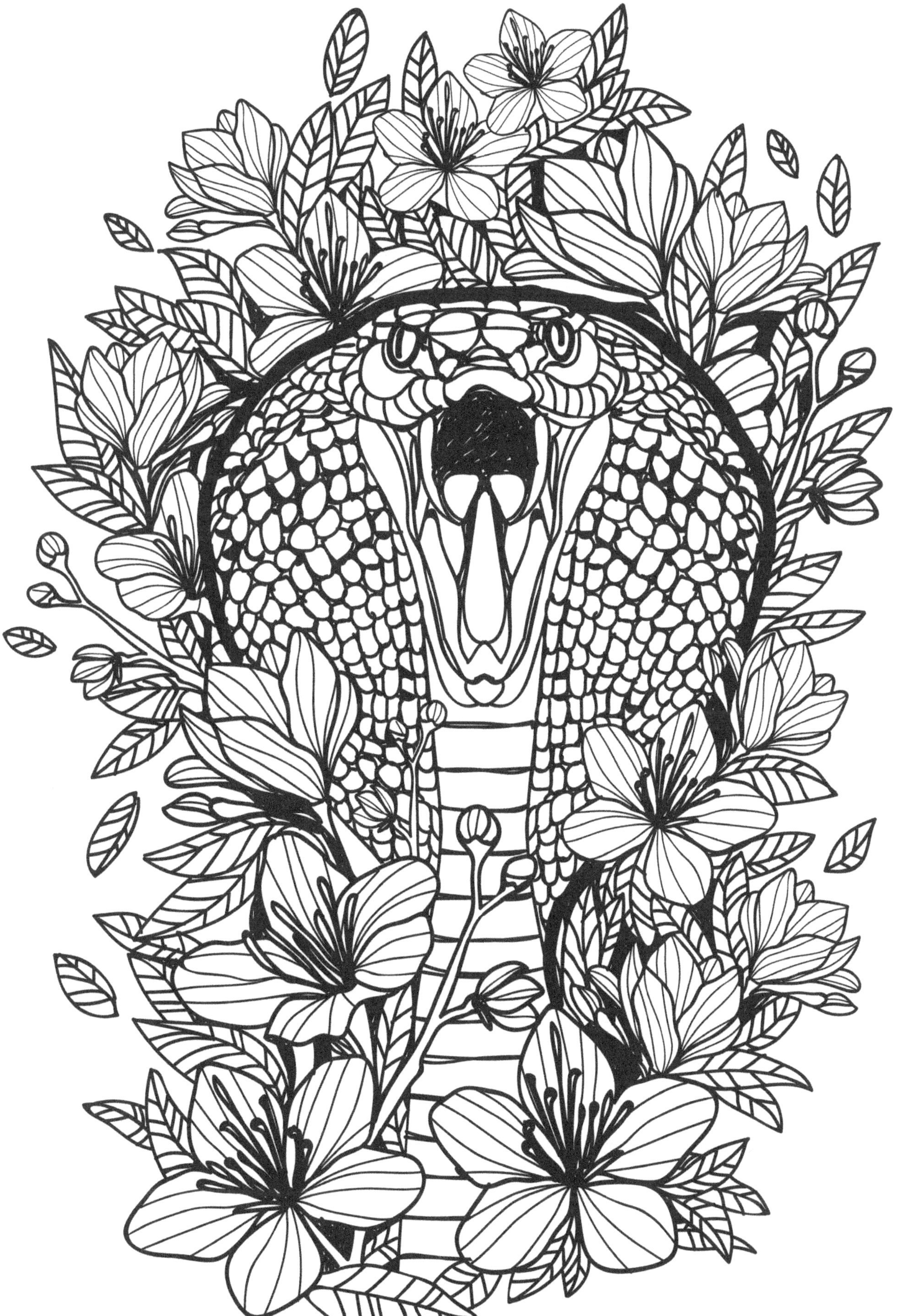

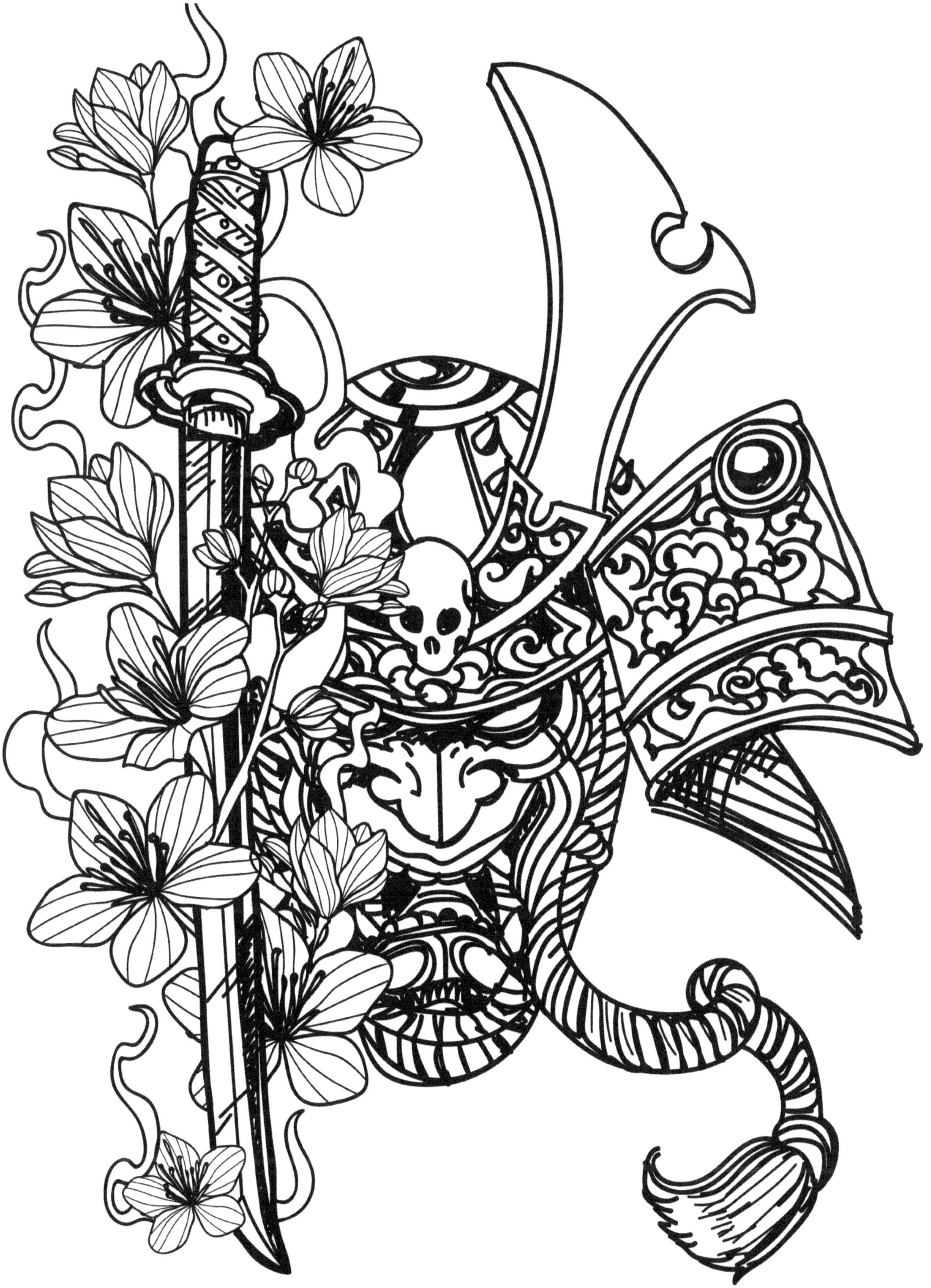

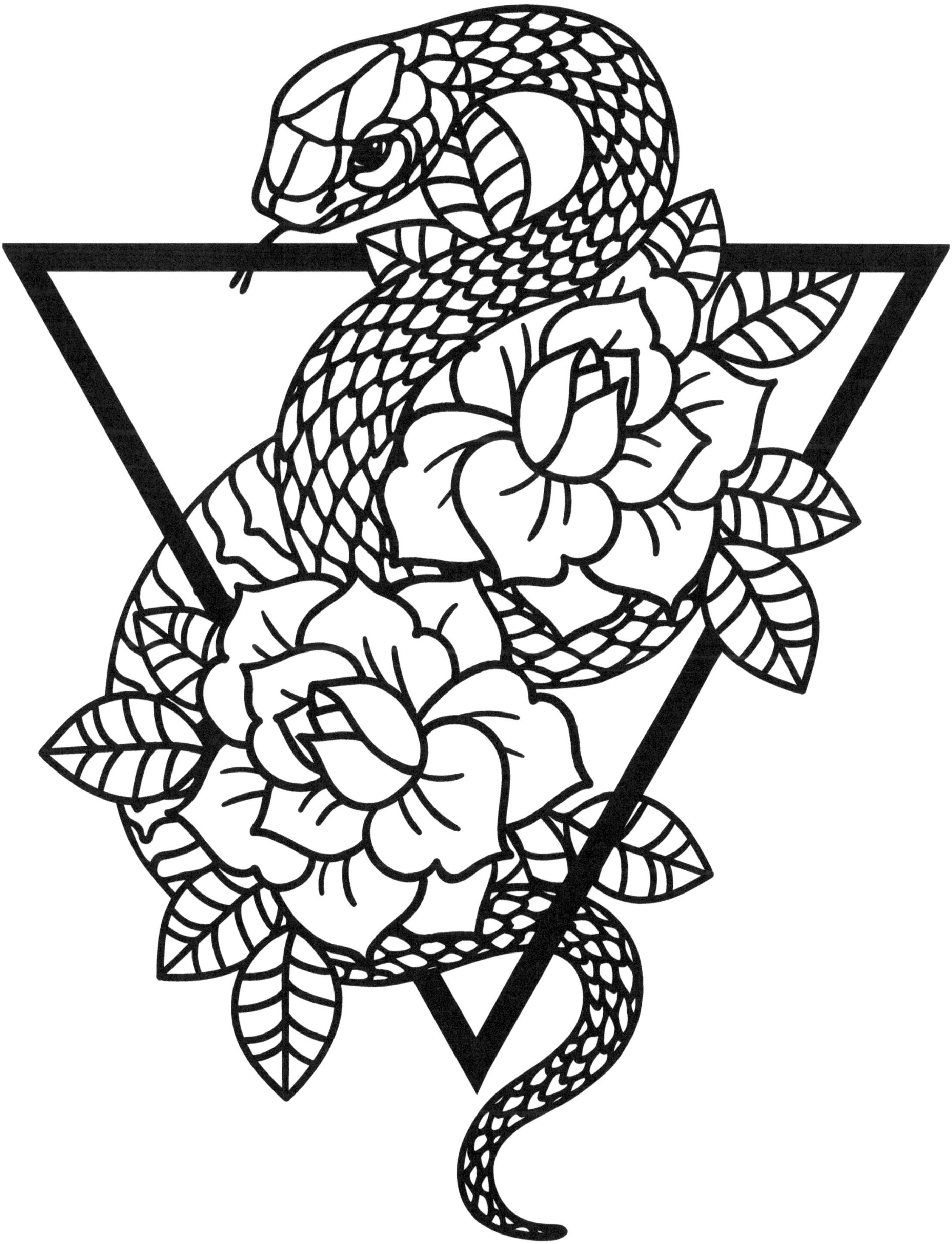

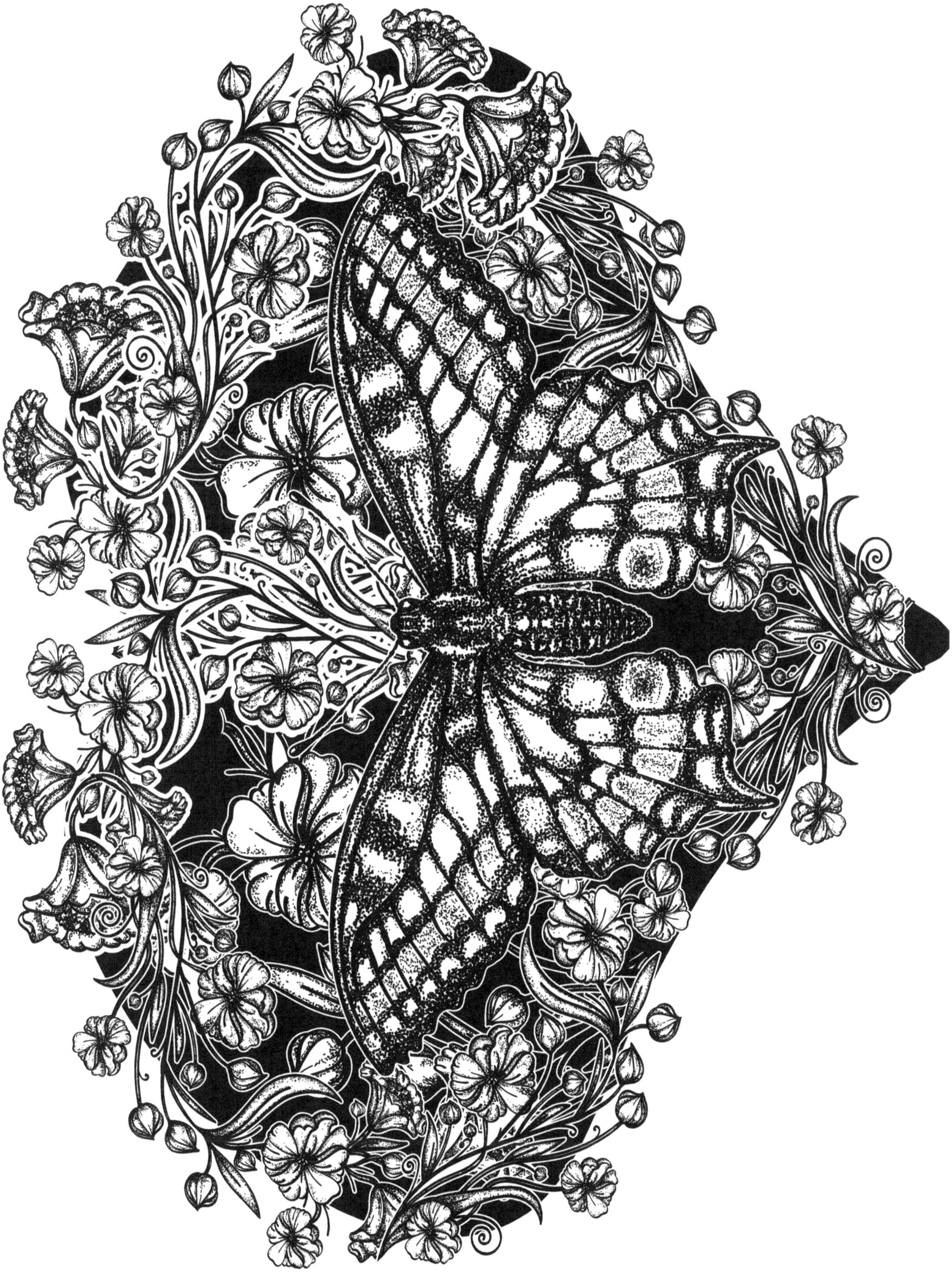

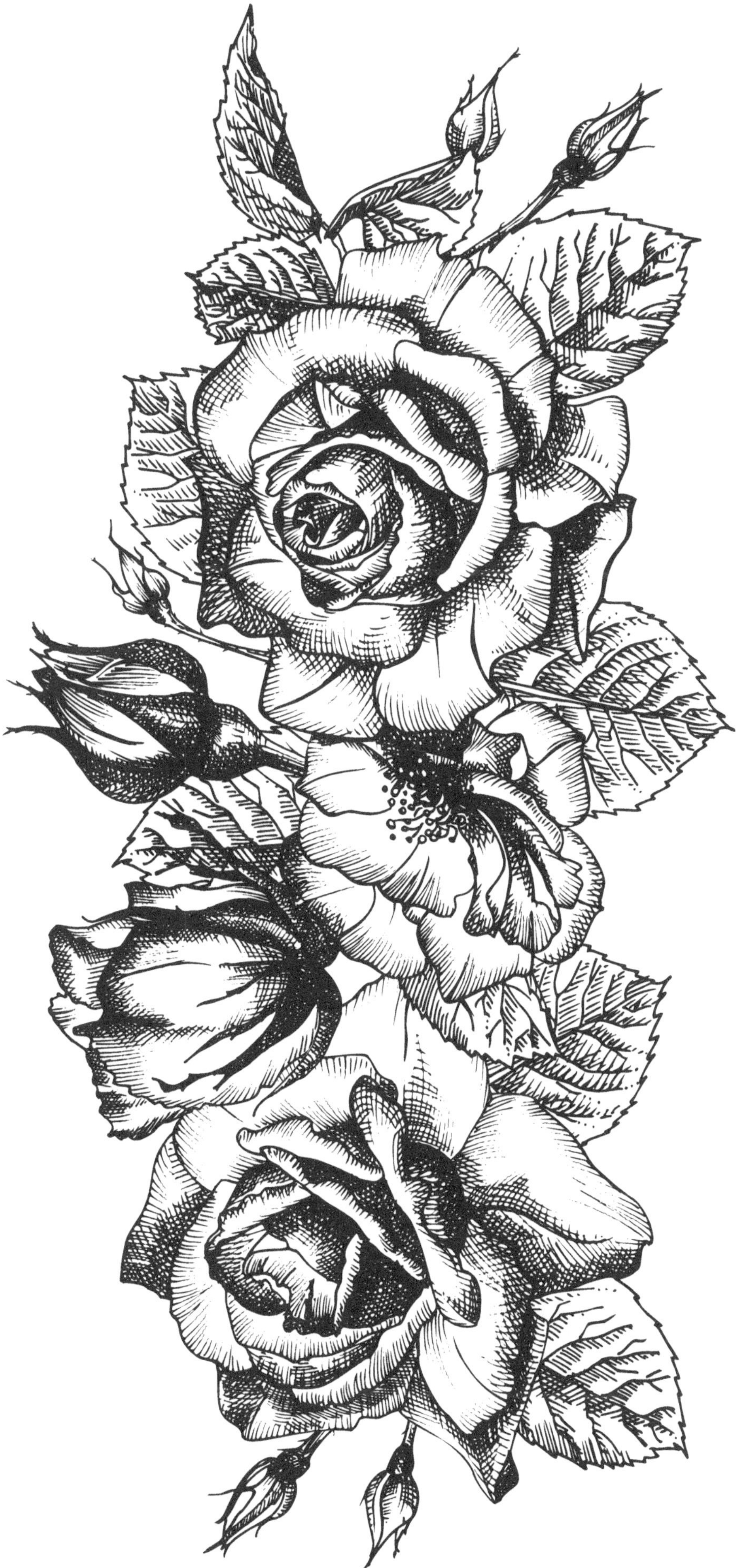

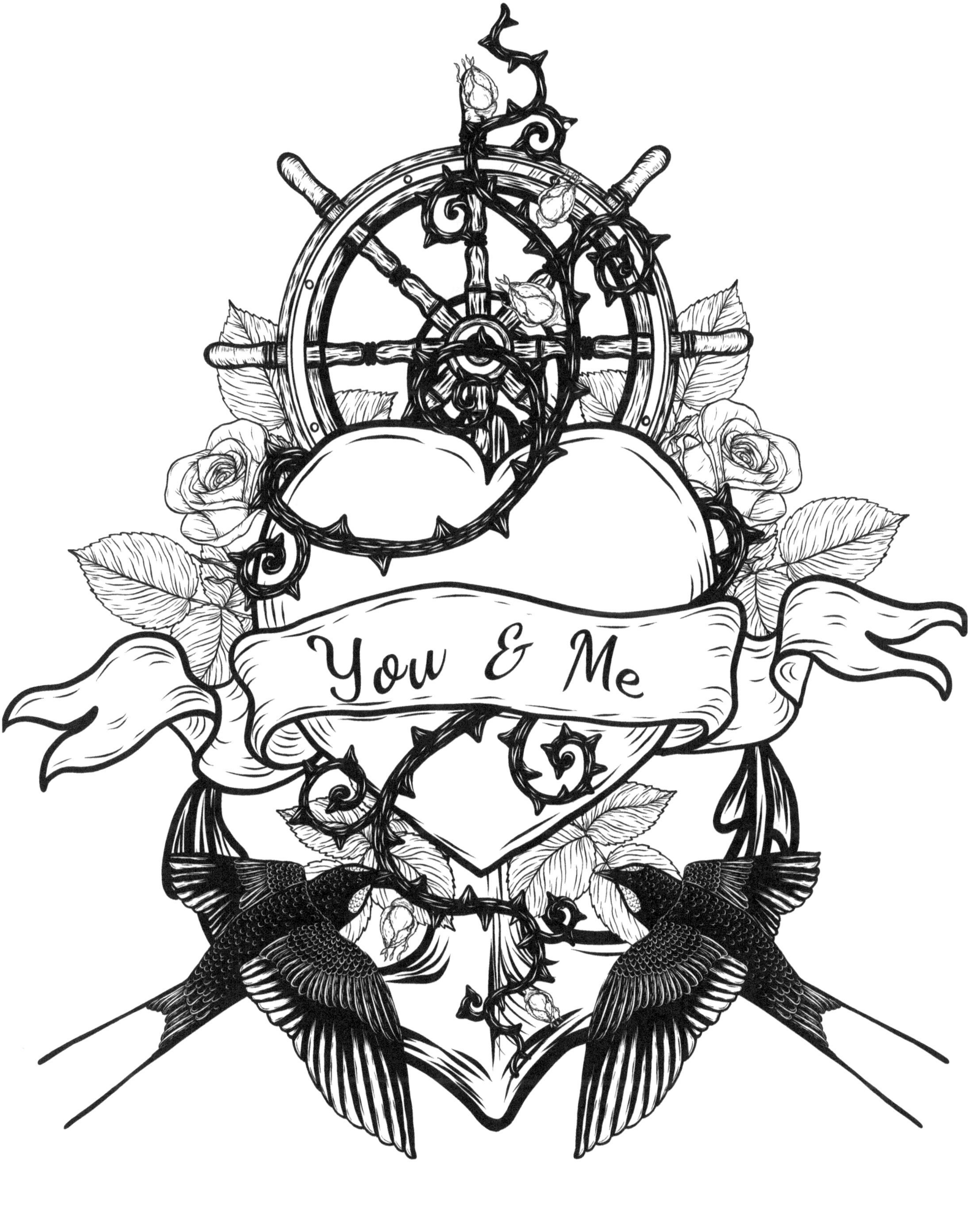
You & Me

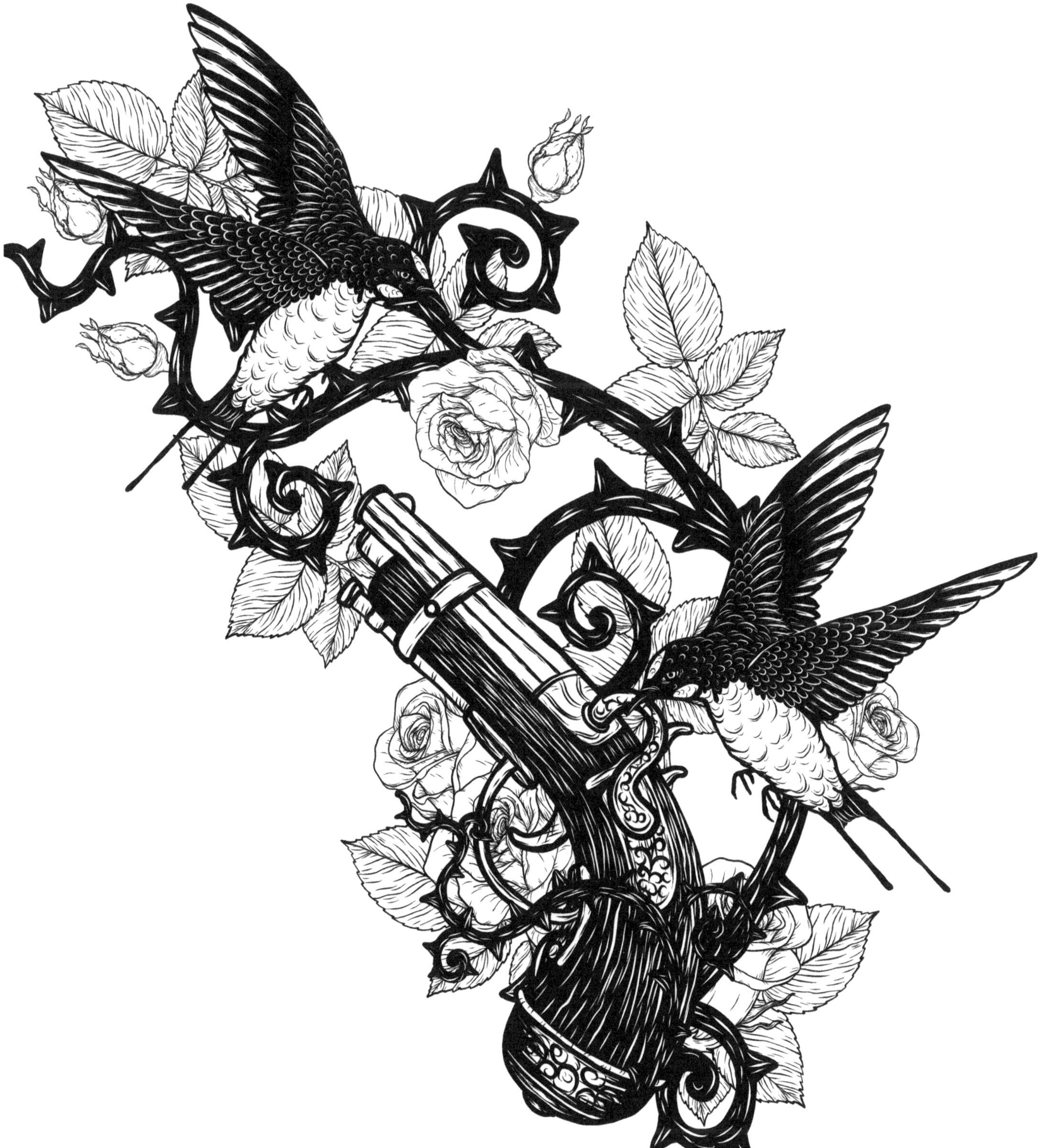

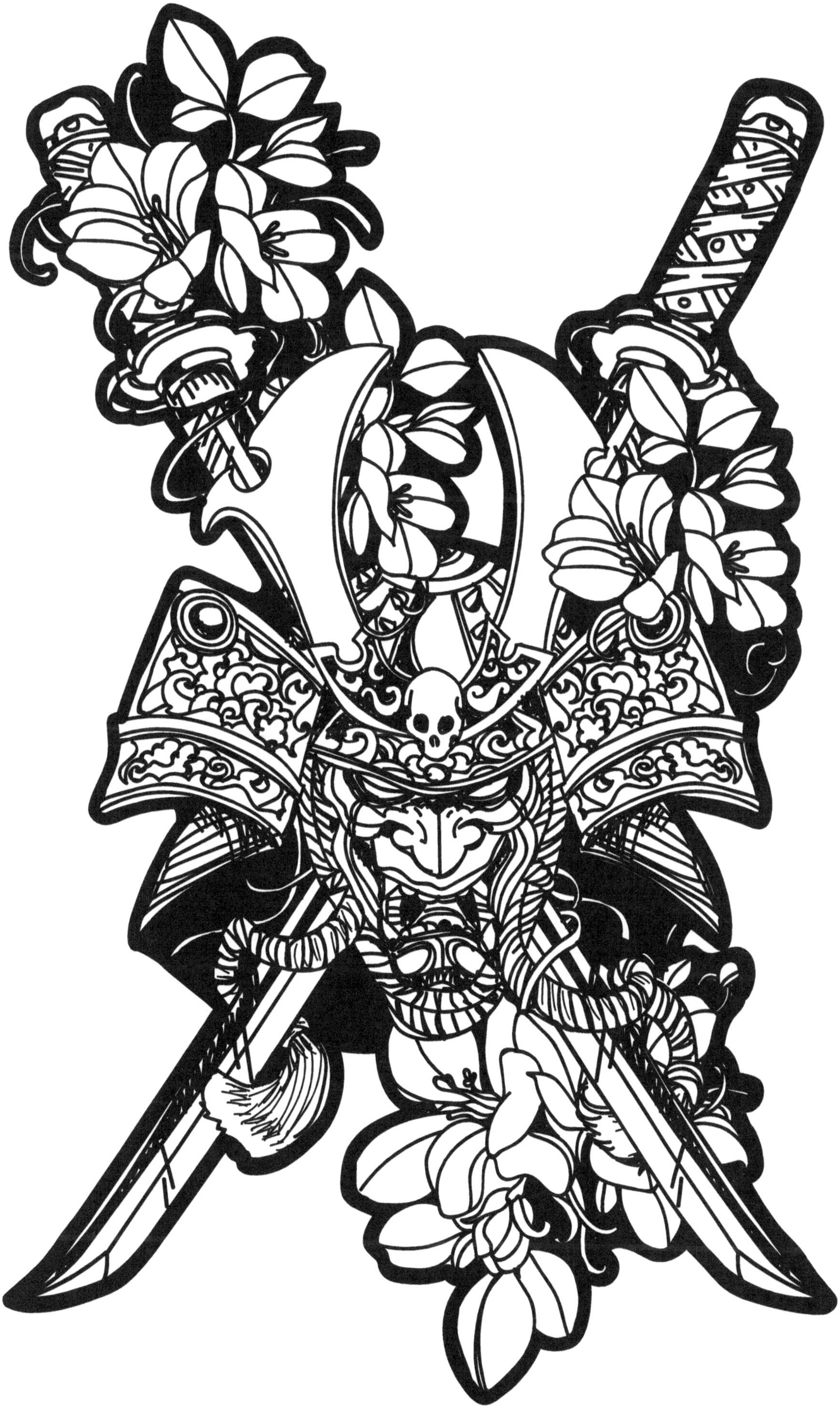

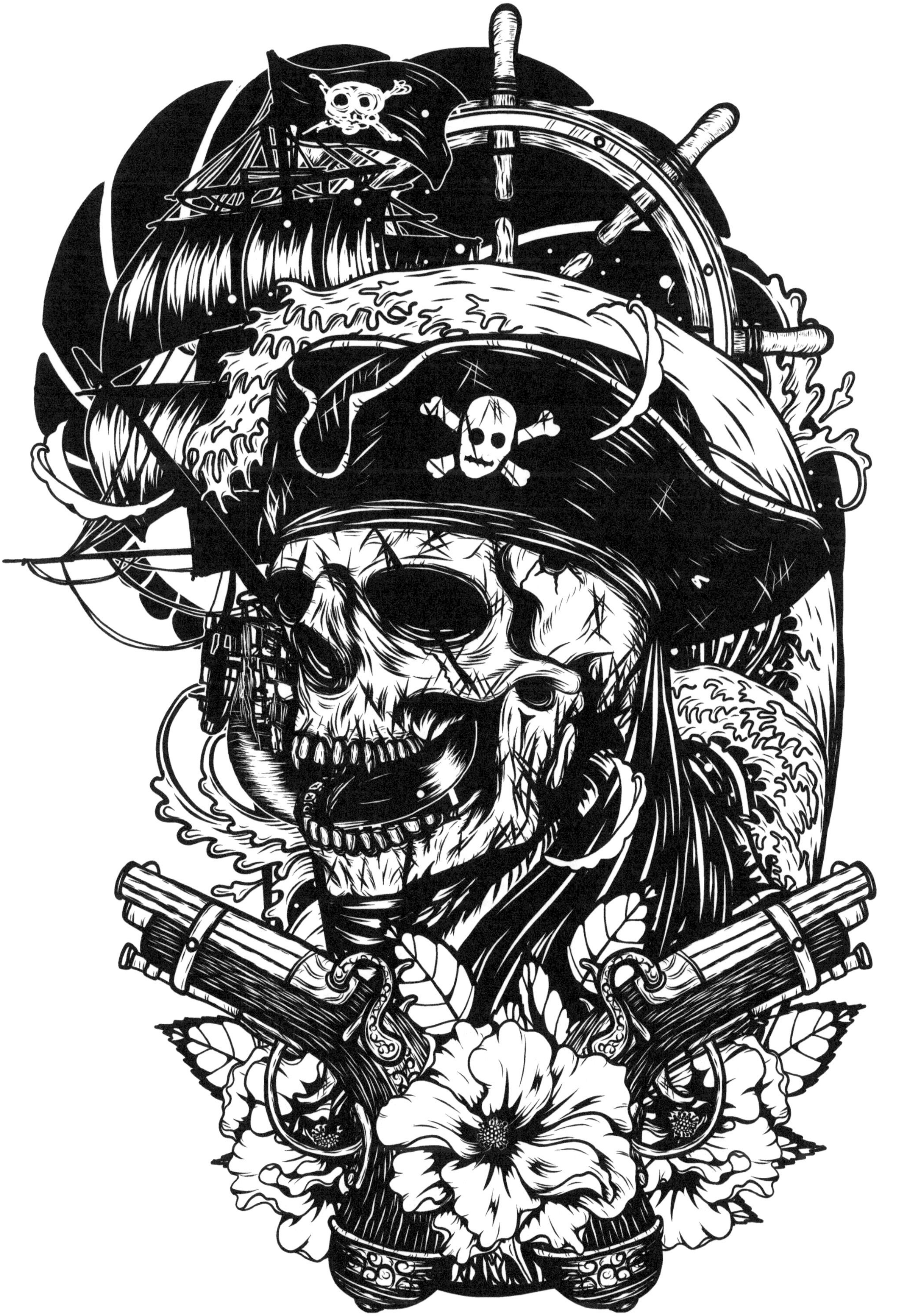

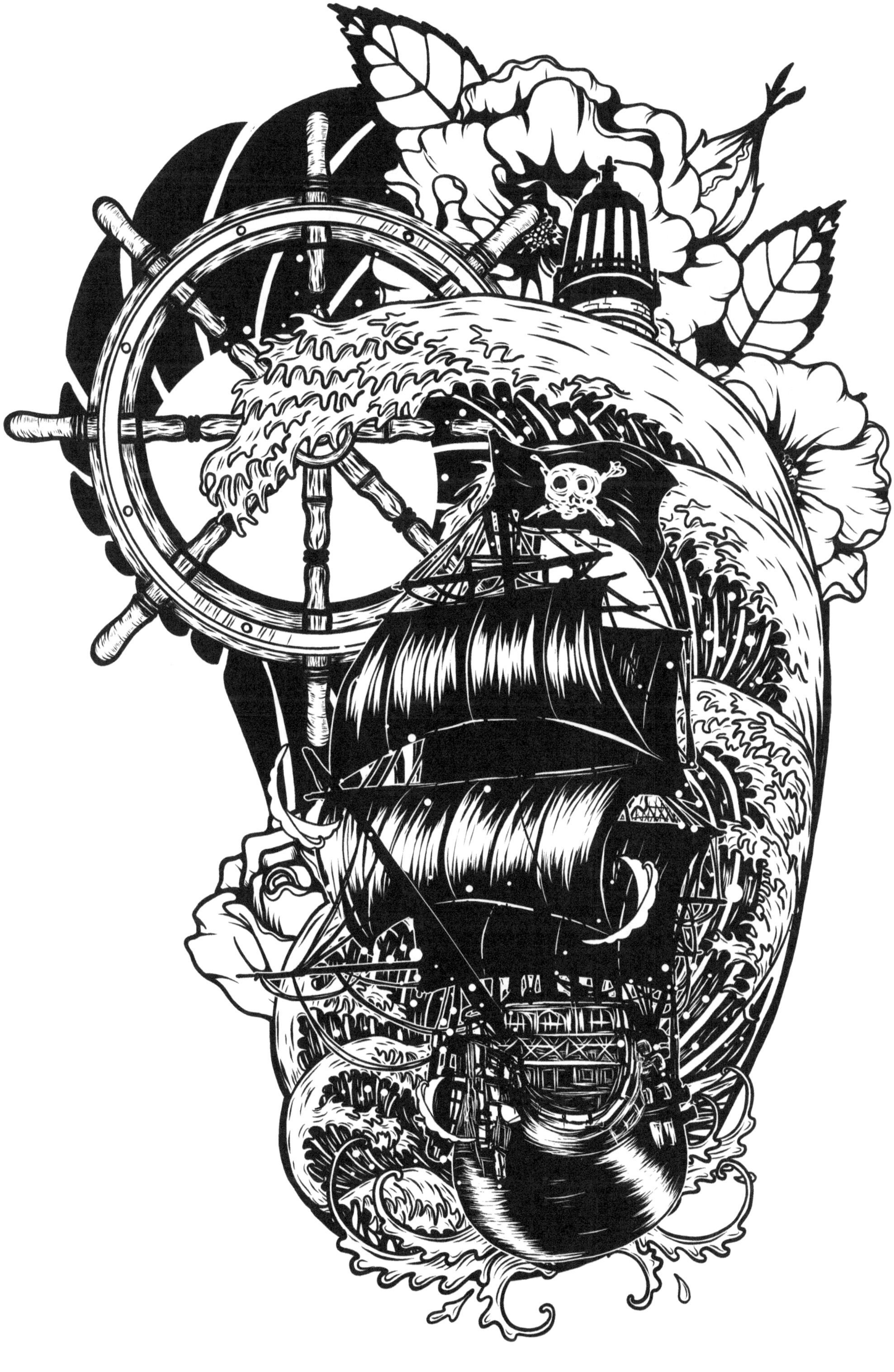

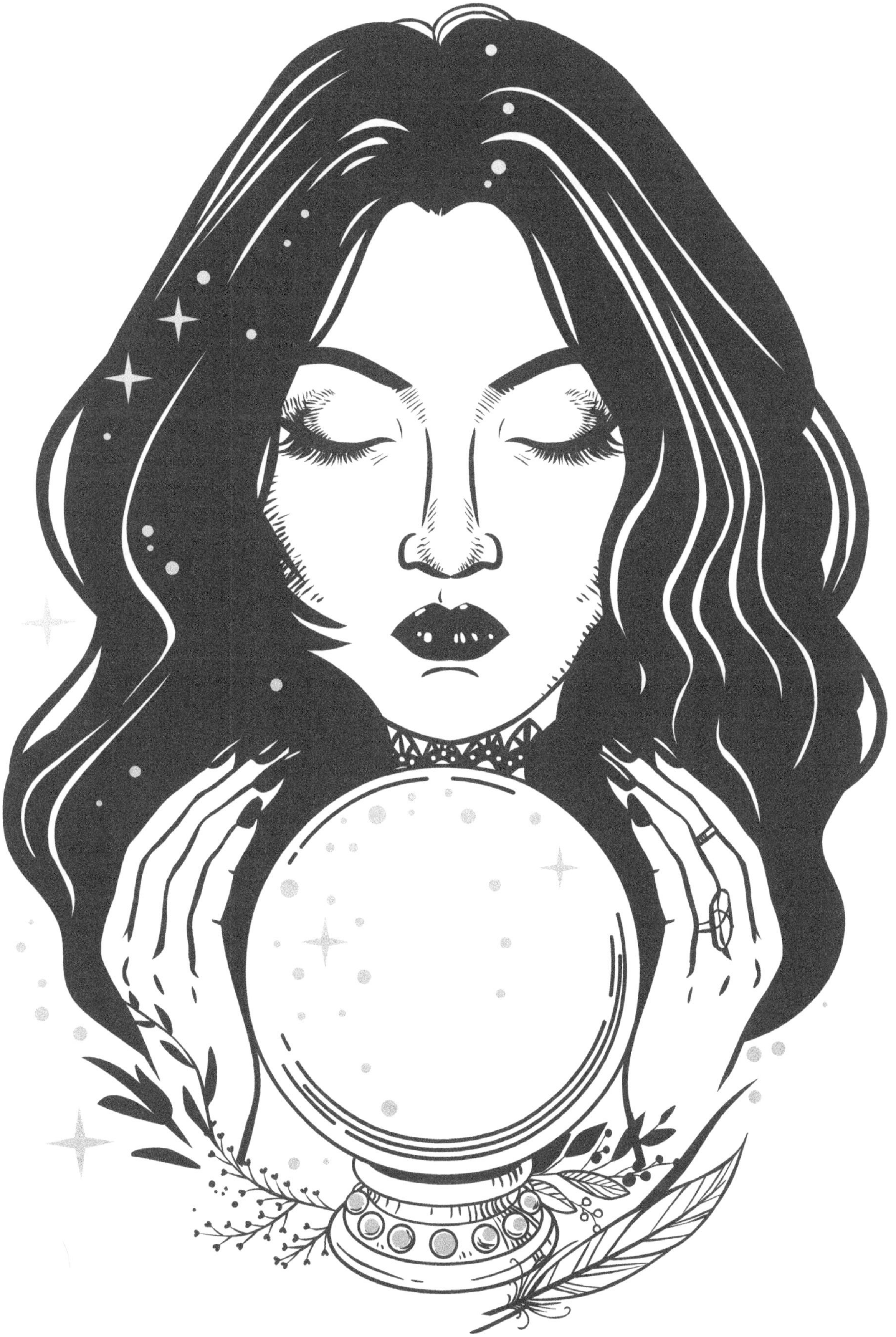

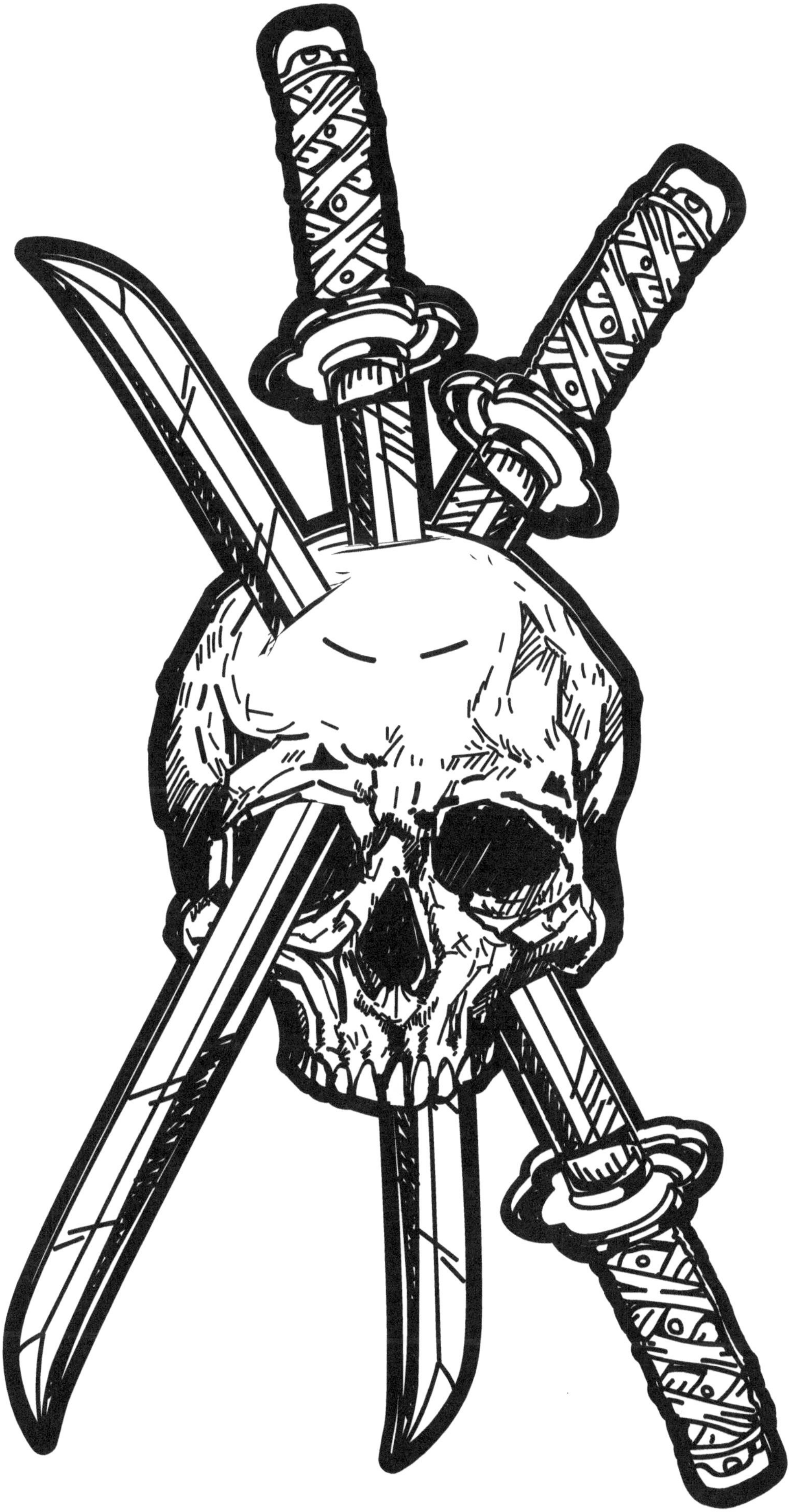

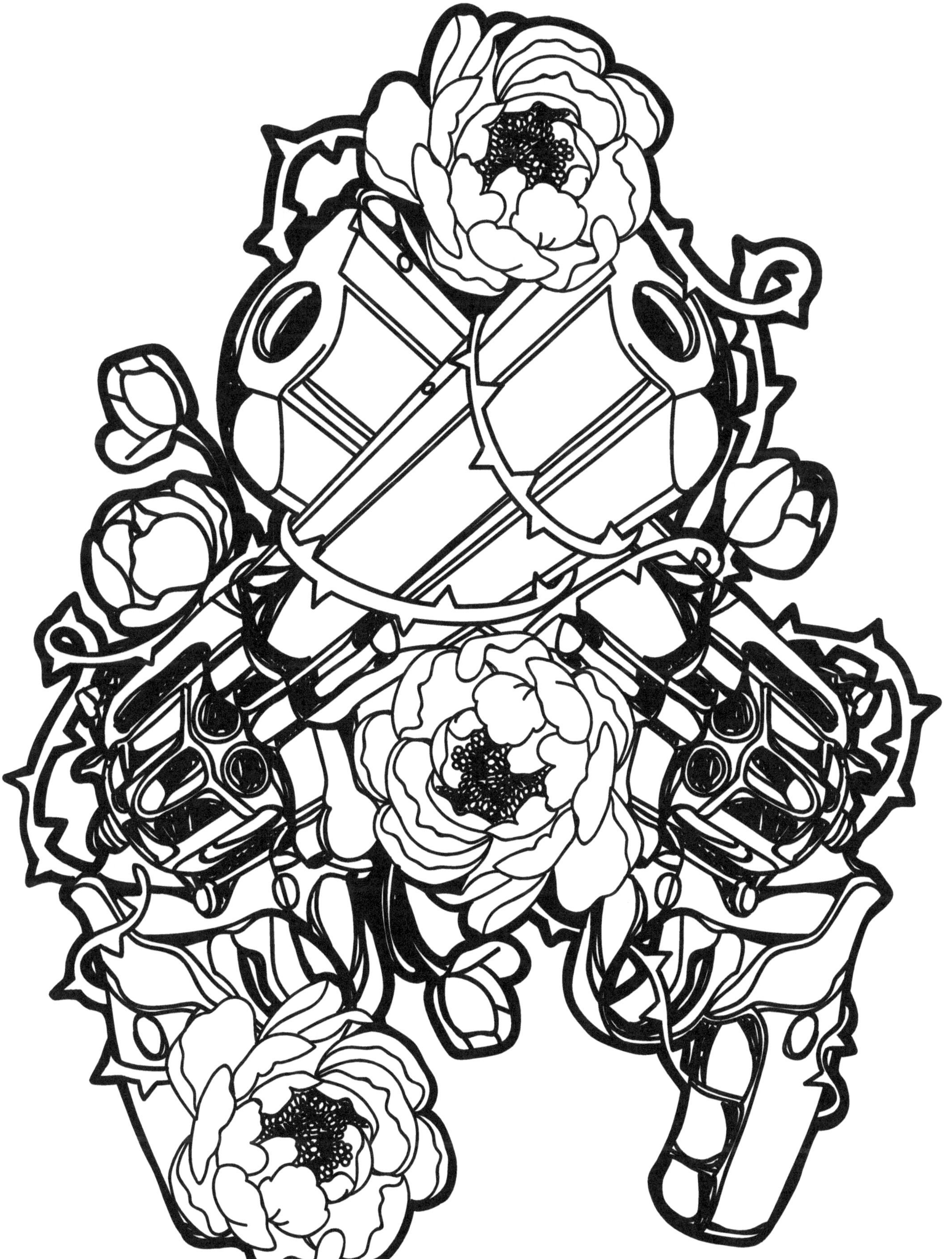

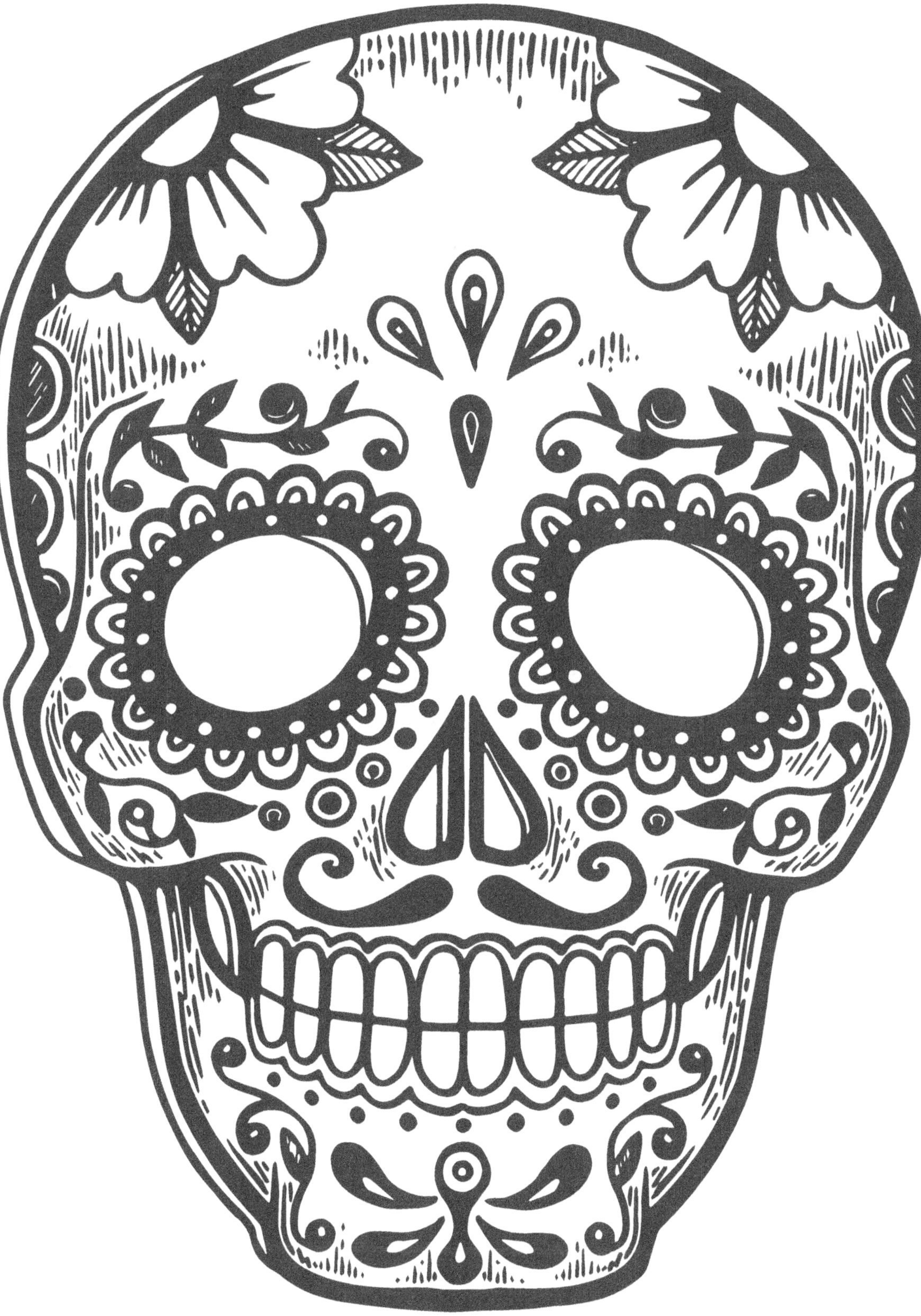

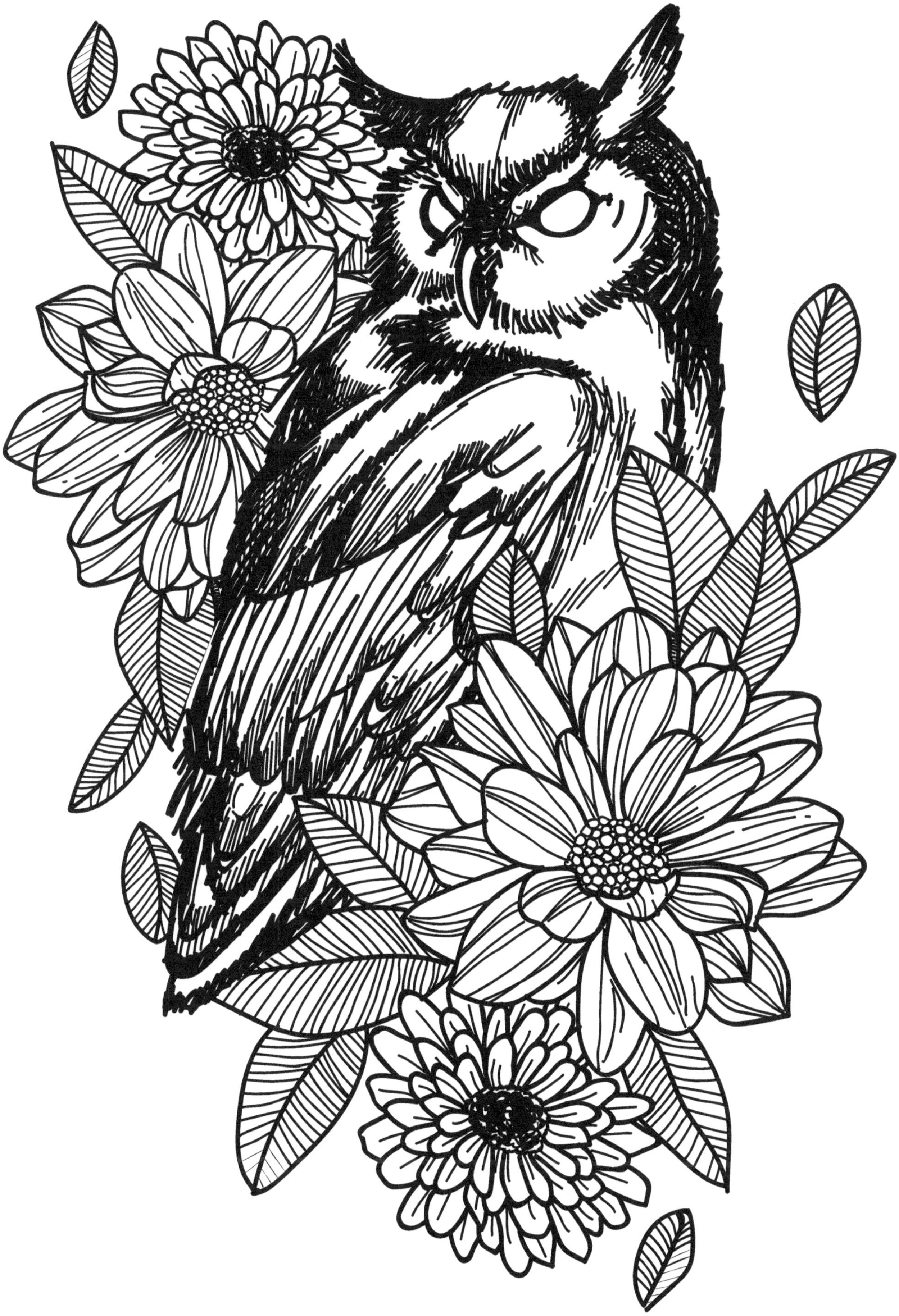

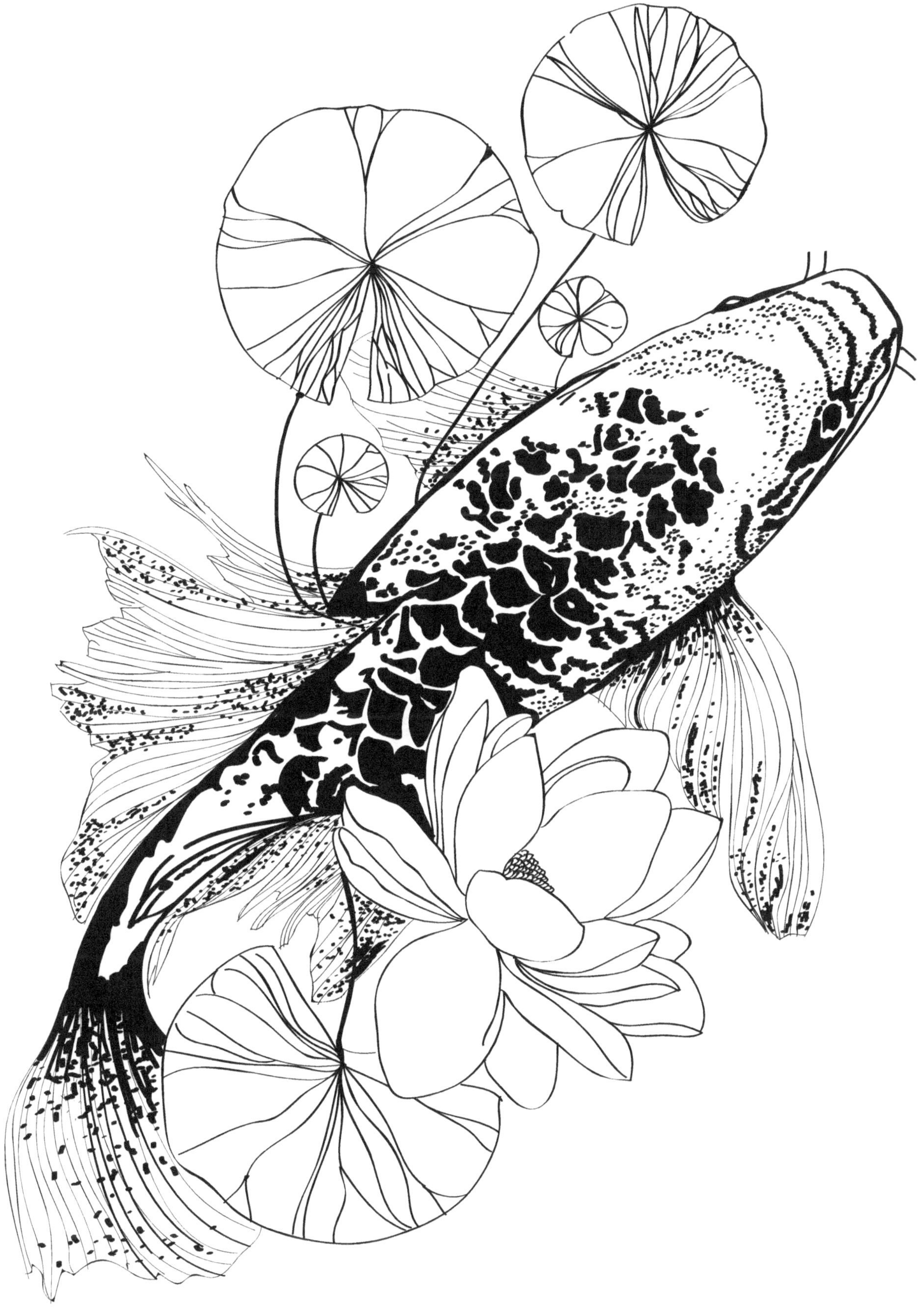

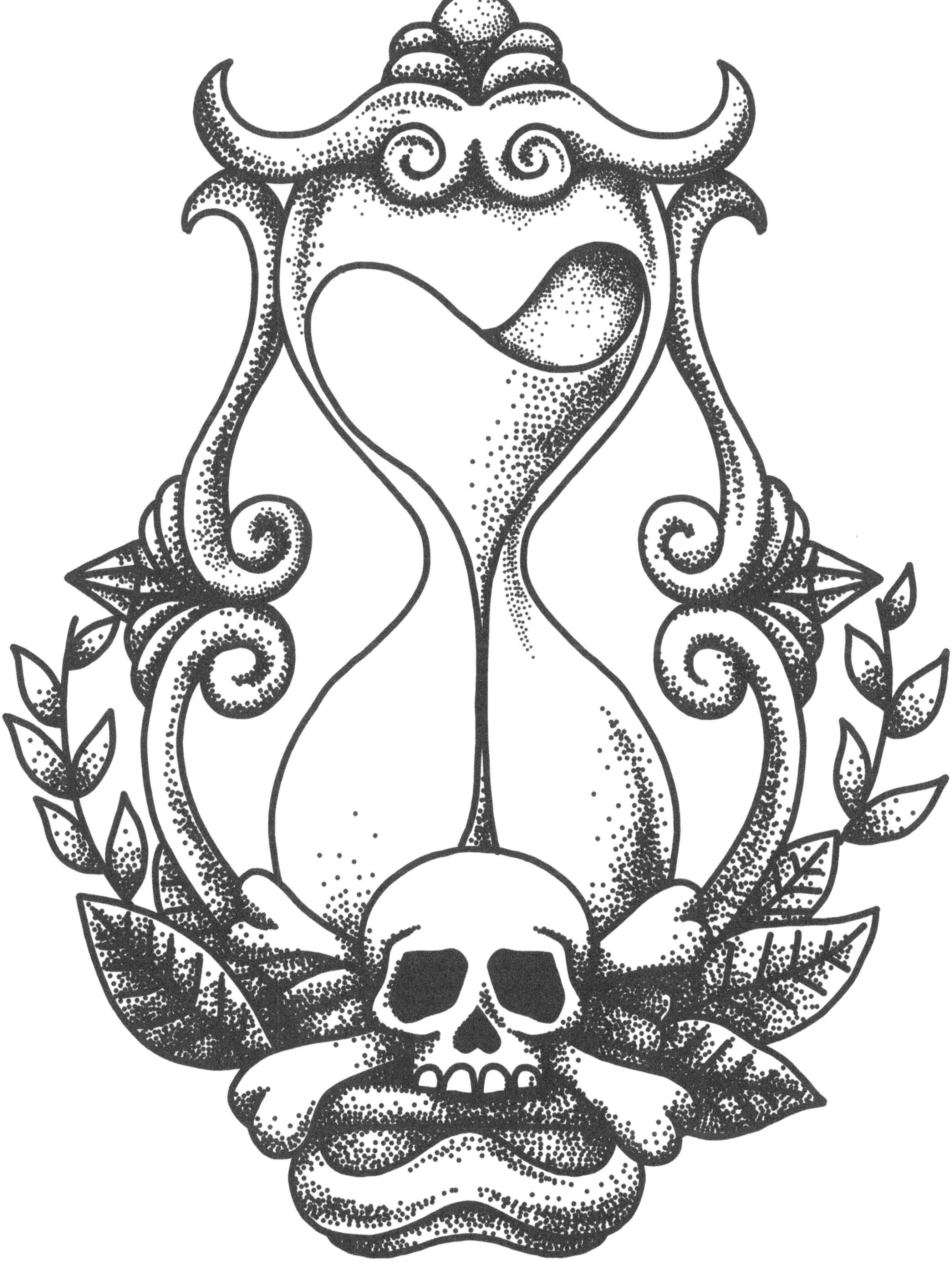

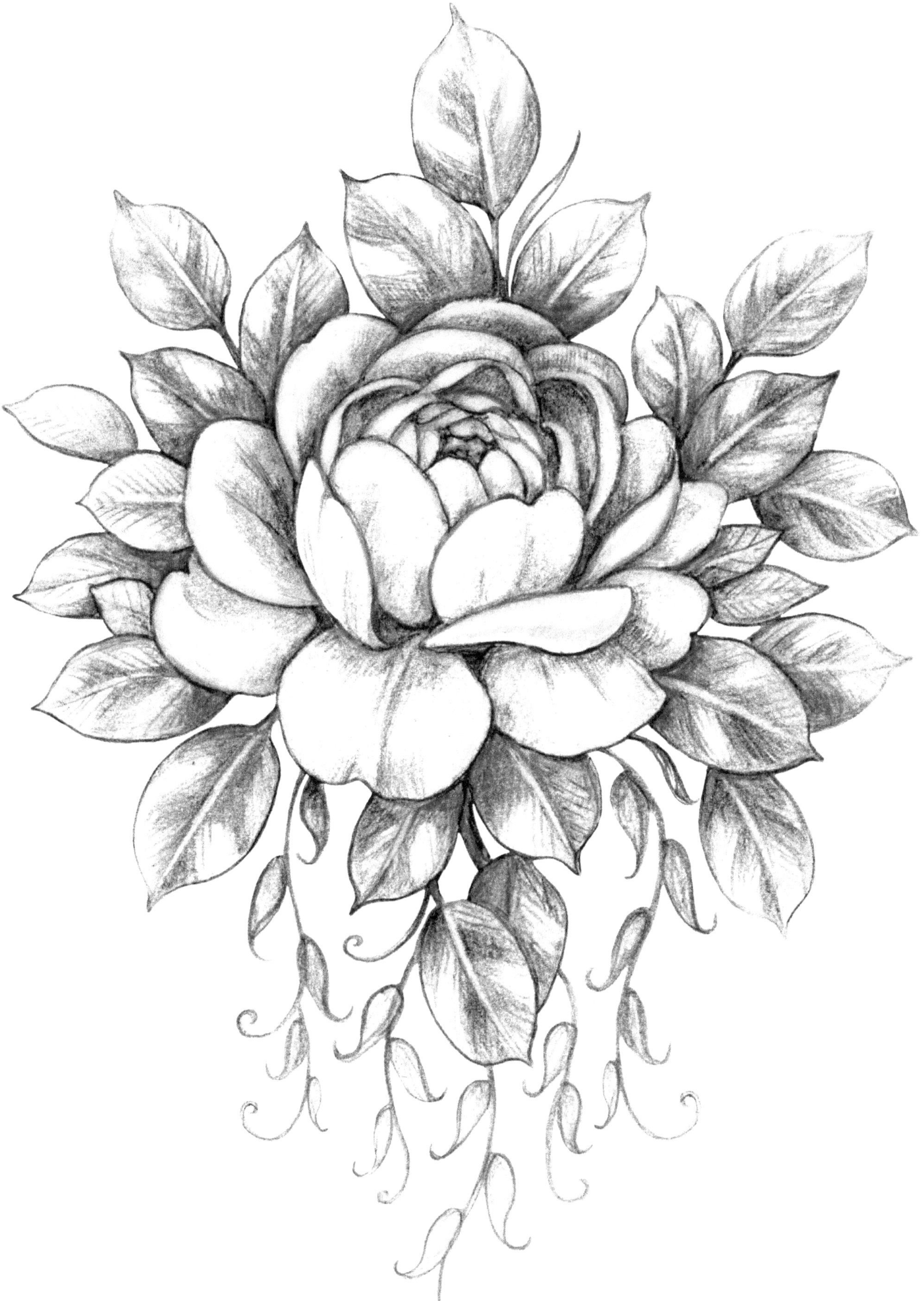

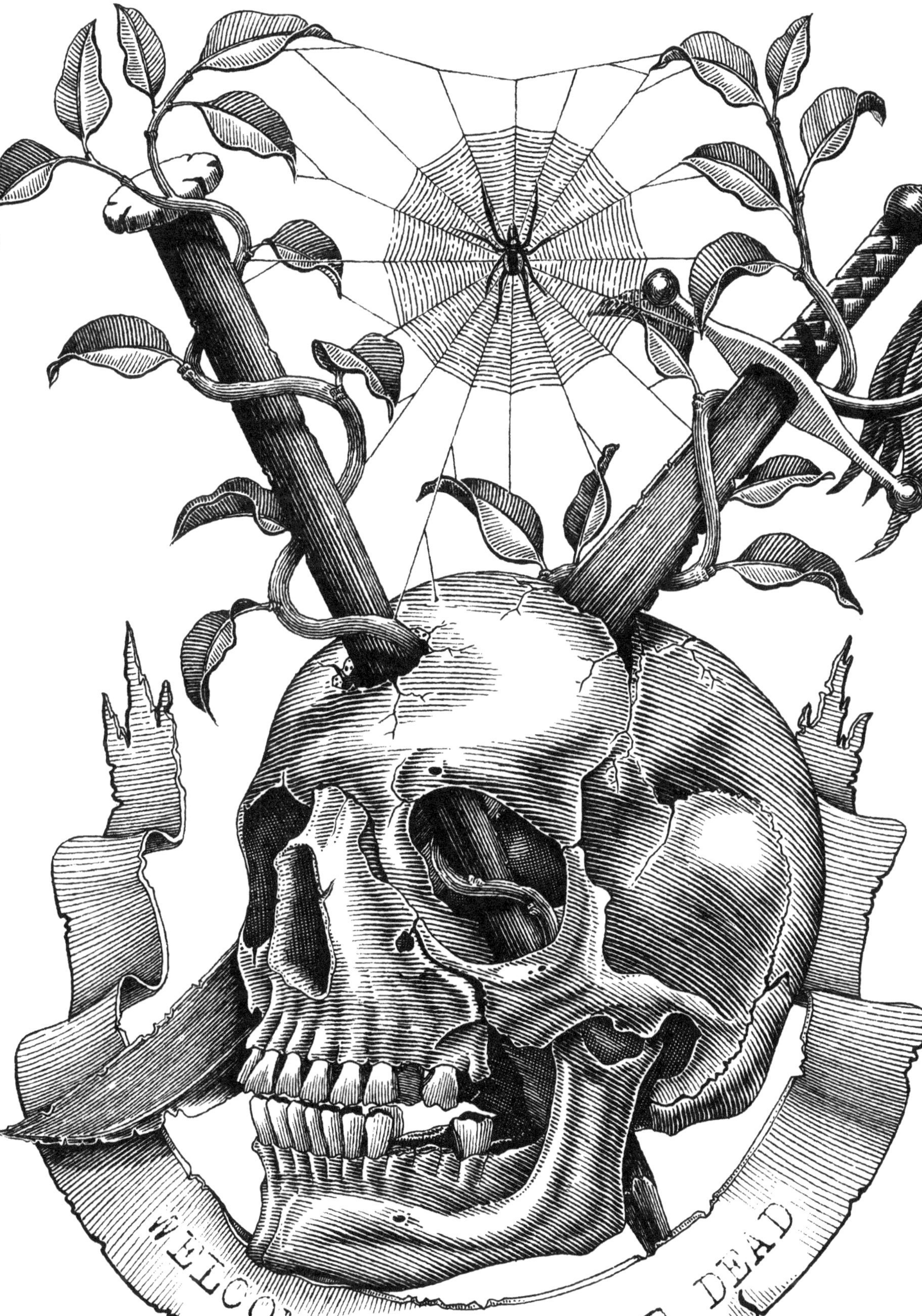
WELCOME TO LAND OF DEAD

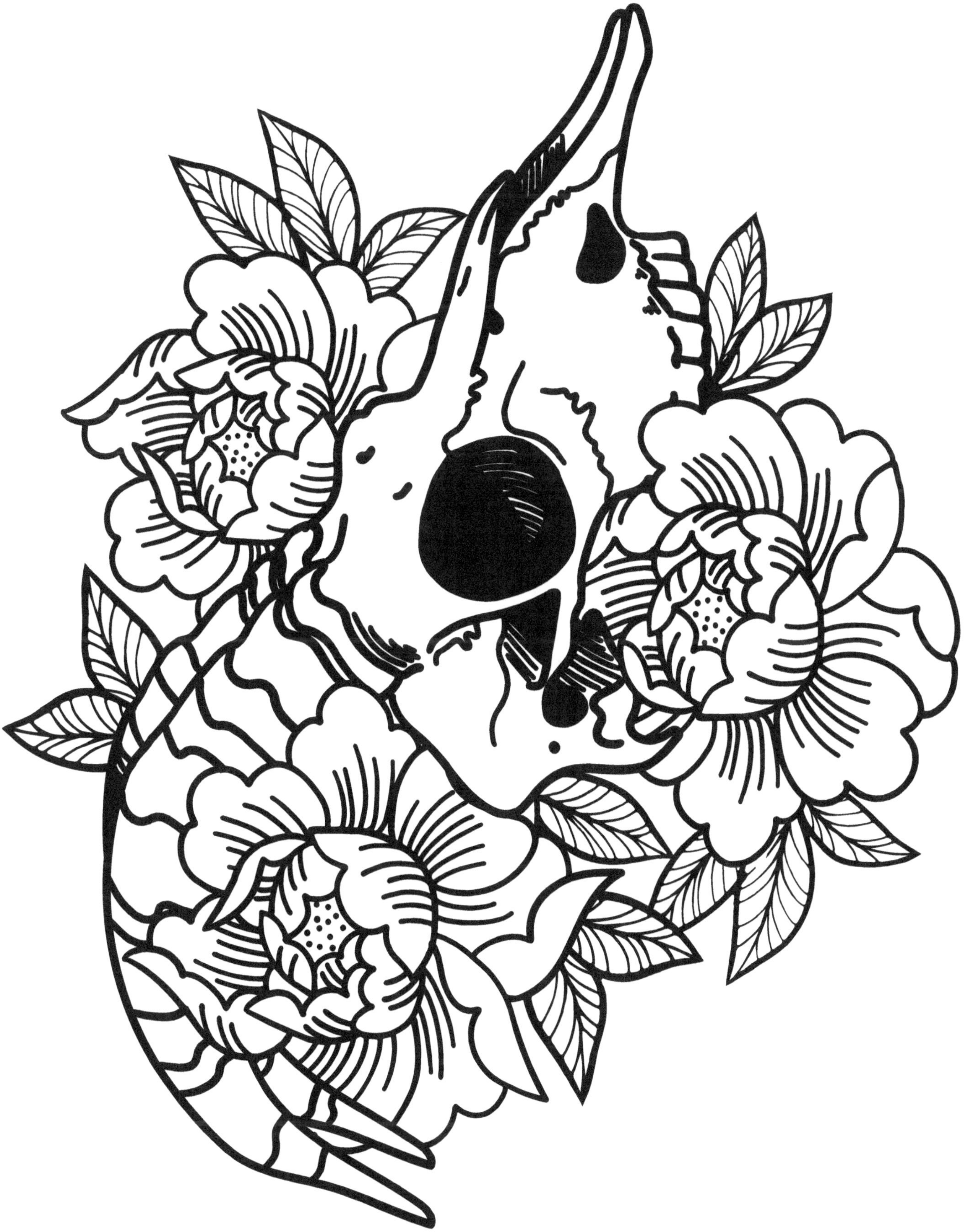

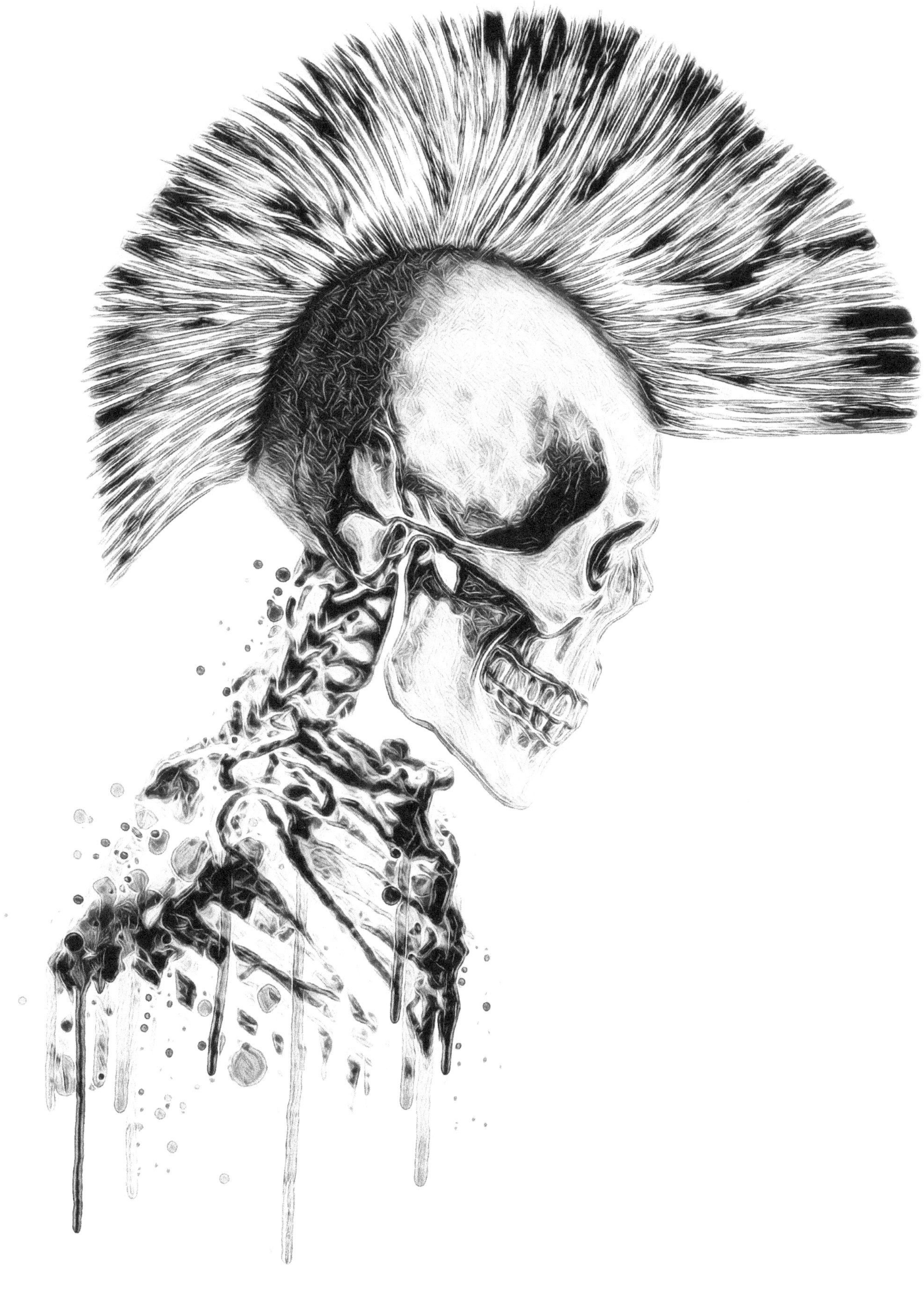

www.ingramcontent.com/pod-product-compliance
Lightning Source LLC
Chambersburg PA
CBHW081004170526
45158CB00010B/2910
9781082430909